Southern Living
Cookbook
Library

The
Ground Beef
Cookbook

Copyright© 1972 Oxmoor House, Inc.
All rights reserved.
Library of Congress Catalog Number: 76–45872
ISBN: 0–8487–0345–6

Cover: Beef Loaf Supreme (page 60)
Left: Hamburger Maximus (page 50)

contents

preface

Ground beef — what a boon for American homemakers and their flavor-appreciating families! It's versatile, adapting nicely to many different roles on your menu, from appetizer to main dish. It's low in cost . . . high in nutrients . . . and mixes and matches with deliciously different sauces, vegetables, and pastas. In fact, it's hard to think of a food more versatile than ground beef. Best of all, ground beef is so popular with every age group that it automatically wins approval as a family-favorite meat.

Southern homemakers — who live in one of our country's great beef-producing regions — know how to make the most of ground beef with flavor-filled, family-pleasing recipes. The very best of these recipes have been assembled here, in *The Ground Beef Cookbook*, for you to serve your friends and family.

As you explore this information-packed book, you'll discover how to prepare great ground beef appetizers . . . soups and stews . . . sandwiches . . . casseroles . . . skillet dishes . . . pies . . . sauces . . . specialty dishes . . . and even quantity dishes. This is the ground beef cookbook you'll depend on again and again. It's full of reliable, home-tested recipes you'll serve with confidence and pride. It's the cookbook certain to enhance your reputation as an excellent cook. From our kitchens to yours, welcome to the wonderful world of ground beef — southern style!

4

Ask any American what his favorite food is and chances are he'll say "steak" or "hamburger" — depending on his age or the state of his pocketbook. We Americans buy more beef than any other kind of meat, and most of us probably eat it for at least one meal a day. Some history buffs think that Americans may have come by their love of beef naturally, as an inheritance from the English. The Yeoman of the Guard — the elite corps which attends the English kings — used to eat so much beef that they were nicknamed "Beefeaters."

AMERICAN CATTLE BREEDS

But the English contribution to America's love for beef isn't limited to an inherited preference for the meat. If it weren't for the last century's pioneer-

introducing beef

ing cattle breeders of England and Scotland, we might not be able today to buy such juicy, tender cuts of beef. In the early 1800's, these explorers began the process of developing new breeds of cattle especially for more tender meat.

Since that time, cattlemen have continued to experiment, breed, and crossbreed so extensively that now there are many fine beef-producing strains. Some of the new breeds you may have heard of are Shorthorn, Hereford, Angus, Brahman, and Santa Gertrudis. Most of the beef sold at local markets comes from these breeds.

The Shorthorn is the oldest of the popular breeds and was brought here from England in 1783, the year that marked the end of the American Revolution. These cattle adapted so well to conditions in our country that today they are the standard breed on many farms. Their color varies from red to white — or may be any combination of the two hues. Some are even a roan color, a blend of red and white hairs. But whatever their color, Shorthorns produce high quality beef.

Herefords were brought to America from England around 1817 by the southern farmer and politician, Henry Clay. This breed is more widely raised in the United States than any other cattle. It is particularly well suited to range country, where it thrives under the harsh environmental influences found in such surroundings. Herefords are a deep rich red color with a white head, breast, and belly, and their compact bodies indicate a high quality of beef.

In 1873 — about fifty years after Henry Clay introduced Herefords — Angus cattle arrived in America. They, too, came from the British Isles, from Aberdeen County in northeastern Scotland. An Angus is easily recognized by its solid black color and its lack of horns.

You may associate the Brahman breed more with rodeos than hamburger steaks, but these cattle are also excellent sources of meat. The American Brahman is a cross between Indian cattle and improved American breeds; it was developed especially to use the grazing land in our hot and humid South and Southwest. With their gray or red hair and hump above their shoulders, Brahmans are a familiar sight on ranches and farms throughout the Southland.

Perhaps the only truly American breed of cattle is the Santa Gertrudis. Developed in the early part of this century on the huge King Ranch in Texas, these cattle are the result of breeding Brahman bulls with purebred Short-horn cows. Santa Gertrudis cattle can adjust to high temperatures — thus they grow and fatten even during the hottest months of the year. These hardy animals are usually solid red with small white markings.

Cattle were roaming in America long before breeding specifically for high quality beef began. The Norsemen brought the first assortment, and, 500 years later, Columbus landed with an Andalusian bull and heifers. Cortez, the Spanish conquistador, made the first significant attempt to raise cattle in the New World. Though many of the cattle he brought from Europe were slaugh-tered for food and leather, when he settled down at Cuernavaca, he raised cattle and originated the Texas Longhorn strain.

A later Spanish explorer, Coronado, hunted treasure in northern Mexico and what is today the southwestern states. Many of his cattle escaped into the brush and eventually were tamed and bred by Spanish missionaries. These Spanish cattle, crossbreeding with native stock, later formed the basis of the herds of many cattle empires which sprung up in Arizona, Texas, and New Mexico.

In the eastern states, cattle became big business after the introduction of the new strains from Britain. Cattlemen moved into the still underdeveloped West and Southwest where there was more room for grazing. The fabulous California Gold Rush in the mid-1800's produced more than precious metal— it added to the need for food. Long after the gold lodes had petered out, the cattle industry kept growing.

And it's still growing today. Right now, the estimated value of cattle roam-ing American farms and ranches is over 13 billion dollars. That's a lot of juicy, nutritious beef on the hoof!

AMERICAN BEEF CONSUMPTION

It's a good thing American cattlemen produce so much beef because the average American eats between 85 and 100 pounds of it every year!

Why does beef make up more than half our meat diet?

Probably because it tastes good and is easy to digest. All year-round it's available in many forms, from fresh steaks to frozen TV dinners and dried beef to hot dogs. Moreover, beef is full of the vitamins, minerals, and proteins needed to keep us active and healthy.

Beef is available all year-round now rather than just after the fall round-up, as used to be the case. With the development of modern refrigeration methods and marketing techniques, beef has become a meat which appears on American tables from January to December.

During the late summer and fall, breeding stock is marketed, primarily for use in processed beef such as hot dogs, bologna, or canned beef. At the same time, range cattle are rounded up and taken to market. Most of these cattle are bought by commercial packers to be fattened before slaughter. They usually gain several hundred pounds in the few months after their diet is changed from range grass to corn or other grains. Finally, steers and heifers which have been bred and fed specifically to develop high quality beef are sold for slaughter.

THE ORIGINS OF BEEF

Ultimately, of course, all the cattle that we see grazing along our highways or stampeding across our television screens go back much further than just a few hundred years. Scholars say that fossil remains of cattle may be as much as three or four million years old. And earlier than that, members of the *Bos* family first appeared on earth. These earliest cattle were huge and shaggy grass eaters with a series of stomachs. Females nursed their young, and bulls fought ferociously. Some skeletons of *Bos primigenius* — the earliest cattle — are six or more feet tall with a span of from ten to eleven feet between their horns!

At some point in history, probably around 10,000 B.C., *Bos* was domesticated by man and has been an important part of his life ever since. Around 8,000 B.C., New Stone Age men took cattle with them on their migrations out of Africa and the Mesopotamia. In the millenia which passed, one's wealth was counted by the number of cattle he owned. Egyptian tombs were decorated with drawings of cattle, some of which were branded with the name or sign of an important god.

Cattle have always played an important part in the mythology and religion of man, from the ancient Egyptians and Hebrews to the Hindus. The Hebraic tribes were constantly warned about getting caught up in popular cults which worshipped cattle — yet even for them, cattle were an important symbol of wealth and food. In India, even in our time, cattle play such a significant role in the religion that they may be treated better than the people who revere them.

GROUND BEEF

Of all the many different meats that come from cattle, perhaps ground beef is one of the most versatile and best-loved. The idea of grinding beef originated in the states which once bordered northern Europe's Baltic Sea. The hardy people who inhabited these areas chopped raw beef with a dull knife

and considered it a luxury food. Later, these same people moved toward Hamburg, one of medieval Europe's busiest seaports. Hamburgers adapted their custom of grinding beef, but preferred it cooked and served on bread.

Hamburgers first made their appearance in the United States at the 1904 World's Fair held in St. Louis. Following their introduction at the Fair, their popularity spread quickly across the country. Soon each region had its own variation of the hamburger — some with sharp seasonings, some with beans or slaw, but all juicy and delicious. Clever American homemakers soon discovered numerous uses for hamburger meat — and a whole range of flavorful recipes was born. The very best of these recipes are highlighted for you in the information-packed pages which follow.

No matter where you buy your ground beef, you can be fairly certain that it's clean and wholesome, came from a healthy animal, and was slaughtered according to Federal regulations. Over 80 percent of the beef sold in American markets is inspected and stamped if it meets Federal standards.

QUALITY

The Federal inspection stamp is important, but so is another Federal stamp, one that certifies quality. The grade of beef you buy has a lot to do with the

FACTS TO AID IN

buying ground beef

flavor and texture of ground beef you serve your family. There are eight grades set up which allow for differences in beef caused by sex, age, health, breeding, feeding, and treatment before and after slaughter. Six of the eight grades can be found in various markets — U. S. Prime, Choice, Good, Standard, Commercial, and Utility. *Prime*, as its name implies, is the finest grade beef. It is often sold only in specialized meat markets. *Choice* is like Prime, but has less fat. *Good* grade appeals to the thrifty shopper. It is low priced and, when cooked properly, can be as flavorful as Prime or Choice. *Standard* beef has little fat and is mild-flavored. *Commercial* beef is far less tender than the first four grades as is *Utility* beef.

Almost any cut of beef can be ground, but ground beef is most often prepared from the less tender cuts that people don't buy in any other form — such as brisket, plate, or shank beef. Ground beef is one of the most versatile kinds of beef and can be roasted, broiled, fried, or combined with many other kinds of foods to make delicious casseroles.

In shopping for ground beef, remember that freshness is the most important quality. Look for the bluish-red color that tells you the ground beef you're examining has been freshly prepared. Most ground beef cannot be kept in the refrigerator more than two days — if you buy day-old ground beef, it should be used right away. The best way to ensure freshness, of course, is to ask your butcher to grind the beef while you wait.

FAT CONTENT

From 15 to 30 percent of ground beef should be fat in order to ensure that the cooked meat will be juicy and tender. Federal regulations limit the amount of fat a retailer can include in the beef he grinds.

Hamburger ranks lowest in grade in the world of ground beef. It may legally contain up to 30 percent fat — and that fat doesn't necessarily have to be all part of the meat being ground. However, hamburger may not contain dry milk, soybean products, cereals, water, or other meat extenders.

Regular ground beef —most often sold simply as "ground beef" —costs a few cents per pound more than hamburger, but usually contains only 20 to 25 percent fat. As a result, it shrinks less when it's cooked. All the fat in ground beef must be part of the cuts being ground, and no extenders of any kind may be added.

Ground chuck is meat cut from the shoulder (or chuck) of the animal. Chuck is a popular cut of beef, and ground chuck is naturally more expensive than hamburger or ground beef. But it's leaner than regular ground beef — only 15 to 25 percent fat. It's especially good for hamburgers.

Ground round is round steak which has been ground. It is extremely lean — only 11 percent fat. For juicier ground round, ask your butcher to add a little ground beef suet to the steak while he is grinding it.

Ground sirloin is prepared from the sirloin cut of steak. It's the most expensive of all ground beef, but the flavor is well worth the extra cost. Ground sirloin is especially good for chopped or Salisbury steaks. It, too, may need to have fat added during grinding.

Meat loaf mixes may be featured in some markets. These are mixtures of ground beef with ground veal and pork and provide a blend of flavors which brings new excitement to an old family favorite.

PRECAUTIONS IN BUYING GROUND BEEF

Because the meat in ground beef is chopped up in very fine bits, bacteria have an infinite number of surfaces on which to multiply and, eventually, to spoil the meat. Plan on using freshly ground beef immediately after you buy it — if you have more than enough for one meal, freeze what you don't use right away. (See the section following for instructions on proper storage of ground beef.)

If you can't be certain about when the ground beef you are purchasing was prepared, don't buy it. And almost as important, if there is any indication that the meat may have been frozen and then thawed for sale, avoid purchase. Meat which has been thawed is even more susceptible to spoilage than day- or two-day-old meat.

When you're planning to serve ground beef, consult this section to determine which type you'll want. Buy it fresh, cook it carefully, and you can be assured of serving your family fresh and flavorful ground beef every time!

Ground beef should always be kept in cold storage and should be handled very little and very carefully because it can be easily contaminated. Ground beef which is beginning to spoil smells like ammonia and has a moist, slightly slimy surface. When ground beef you are storing develops these characteristics, it should be discarded immediately.

REFRIGERATOR STORAGE

Store freshly ground beef in the coldest part of your refrigerator — right underneath or over the freezer compartment if you have room. Beef stays fresh longer when some air circulates around it. If your ground beef is

storing ground beef

wrapped in butcher's paper or plastic wrap, loosen the wrapping slightly before storing the meat. The maximum length of time you can safely store ground beef in the refrigerator is two days. If you need to store it longer than that time, plan on freezing it.

FREEZER STORAGE

Ground beef to be frozen should go into the freezer immediately after purchase — storing it in the refrigerator for a day or two prior to freezing may permit spoilage to begin. For the safest freezing, your freezer should maintain a temperature of zero degrees or lower. If your freezer maintains this temperature, you can plan on keeping ground beef for up to four months. But if it doesn't, don't store ground beef for more than two weeks at a time.

Prepackaged beef can be safely frozen in its original wrapping for up to two weeks, as long as there are no breaks in either the wrapping or the tray. For longer periods of storage, add an outer wrapper of freezer paper. Ground beef which is not prepackaged should be wrapped in moisture/vapor proof paper — such as aluminum foil or plastic wrap. (Waxed paper doesn't work.)

Don't try to freeze too many packages of ground beef at once. Each package should have some contact with the freezing surface. If you try to stack packages, those in the middle will freeze more slowly than those on the top and bottom — and will lose flavor.

Ground beef may be thawed at room temperature, but don't allow it to stand unfrozen at this temperature for long. Or you may take it from your freezer and thaw it in your refrigerator. Allow about one to two hours' thawing time per pound.

Beef not only tastes good, it keeps you feeling alert and energetic because it supplies a very high quality protein. This protein is called a "complete protein" because it contains all twenty-one of the amino acids the body needs for growth and the maintenance of body tissues.

Beef is also a good source of Vitamin A and the vitamins in the B group, including all-important riboflavin and niacin. Moreover, beef provides essential minerals like iron, copper, and phosphorus in a form the body can readily use.

The chart below details the nutrients provided by beef and the ways in which the body uses them.

BEEF
nutrition chart

NUTRIENT	ROLE IN BODY CHEMISTRY
Iron	Helps make hemoglobin (the red pigment in blood) and carry oxygen to tissues
Phosphorus	Forms bones and teeth
Copper	Forms hemoglobin
Sodium, Potassium	Helps regulate bodily functions
Vitamin A	Promotes growth and repair of body tissues, builds good health, maintains normal vision and healthy eyes, keeps skin soft and mucous membranes healthy
Vitamin B_1 (thiamine)	Important in the transformation of carbohydrates to energy forms the body can use and in the normal functioning of heart, nerves, and muscles
Vitamin B_2 (riboflavin)	Maintains good vision, builds healthy skin and mouth tissues, aids in the conversion of carbohydrates to energy forms
Niacin	Builds and maintains healthy skin and mucous membranes, aids in the use of carbohydrates and in the healthy functioning of the nervous system
Vitamin B_6 (pyridoxine)	Helps the body use amino and fatty acids
Vitamin B_{12}	Necessary for the formation of red blood cells and the proper functioning of the brain

Basil Meatballs (page 23)

appetizers

Preface your meal — or that enjoyably relaxed party — with great appetizers. Southern homemakers, who enjoy entertaining their families and friends, know that appetizers give every get-together a special flair. They are conversation starters, ice breakers, and marvelous palate-pleasers!

Ground beef with its flavors that blend with light or hot seasonings and its smooth texture is a natural choice for quick and easy appetizers. This versatile meat takes on many exciting forms in .dips, meatballs, tiny cocktail pizzas, and even in just-right salads.

Star ground beef appetizers at your next gathering. Serve Hamburger Biscuit Roll — flaky light biscuits with a hot and hearty filling . . . Spicy Meat-filled Pastries . . . Chafing Dish Meatballs . . . and a party-perfect Ground Chuck Fondue! Even though all these appetizer recipes use ground beef, each one tastes different.

You may decide to let ground beef form the basis of your salad — imagine the compliments you'll receive when you present Hot Mexican Salad to your appreciative friends and family.

These are just some of the home-tested, family-approved ground beef appetizer recipes waiting for you in the pages that follow. For flavor, versatility, and economy, you'll find ground beef appetizers can't be excelled!

Hot and Hearty Dip (below)

HOT AND HEARTY DIP

1 lb. ground beef
1 1 1/2-oz. envelope seasoning
   mix for Sloppy Joes

1 6-oz. can tomato paste
1/2 c. sour cream

Brown the beef in a skillet and stir in the remaining ingredients, blending well. Bring to a boil, then reduce the heat. Cover and simmer for 5 minutes, stirring occasionally. Serve hot with crackers or corn chips. About 2 cups dip.

SOMBRERO HOT DISH

1 lb. ground beef
1/2 c. chopped onion
2 8-oz. cans red kidney beans
1/2 c. hot catsup

3 tsp. chili powder
1 tsp. salt
1 c. shredded sharp cheese

Brown the ground beef and onion in skillet. Mash the beans with a fork in the liquid. Add the beans, catsup, chili powder and salt to the beef mixture and blend well. Cook until bubbly. Pour into a 2-quart chafing dish and sprinkle the cheese over the top. Serve hot with corn chips.

Mrs. Carolyn Butler, Rocky Mount, North Carolina

BEEF PICADILLO

1/2 lb. ground beef	3/4 c. diced pimento
1/2 lb. ground pork	3/4 c. toasted almonds
1 tsp. salt	2 1/2 cloves of garlic, minced
1/4 tsp. pepper	1 6-oz. can tomato paste
4 tomatoes, peeled and diced	2 jalapeno peppers, chopped
3 green onions, finely diced	3/4 c. seedless raisins
3 med. potatoes, diced	1/4 tsp. oregano

Cover the beef and pork with water and add the salt and pepper. Simmer, covered, for 30 minutes, then add remaining ingredients. Cook until potatoes are tender. Remove the excess fat. Serve in a chafing dish with corn chips. 20 servings.

Mrs. John E. Mitchell, Jr., Memphis, Tennessee

PIZZA FONDUE

1 onion, chopped	1 1/2 tsp. oregano
1/2 lb. ground beef	1/4 tsp. garlic powder
2 tbsp. shortening or margarine	2 10 1/2-oz. cans pizza sauce
1 tbsp. cornstarch	10 oz. Cheddar cheese, grated
1 1/2 tsp. fennel seed	1 c. grated mozzarella cheese

Brown the onion and beef in shortening in fondue pot over high heat, then reduce the heat to medium. Combine cornstarch, seasonings and pizza sauce and stir into the beef mixture, mixing well. Cook until thick and bubbly. Add the cheeses by thirds, stirring well after each addition. Adjust to medium heat to maintain bubbly consistency to serve. Serve with garlic bread cubes or toasted English muffin cubes for dunking. May be prepared in saucepan on stove.

Mrs. Mary Shopner, Athens, Georgia

HAMBURGER BISCUIT ROLL

1 lb. ground beef	Salt and pepper to taste
1/2 c. minced onion	1/4 to 1/2 c. chili sauce
1/4 c. minced green pepper	1 recipe biscuit dough

Combine ground beef, onion and green pepper in skillet and saute until lightly browned. Pour off fat. Mix in salt, pepper and enough chili sauce to make of spreading consistency. Divide dough in half and roll each half into rectangle, 1/2 inch thick. Spread each rectangle with meat mixture. Roll up, beginning at wide side. Seal by pinching edges of the dough together. Place seam side down, on greased baking sheet and pierce with fork to let steam escape. Bake at 425 degrees for about 20 minutes. Cut into 1/2 to 1-inch thick slices and serve warm.

Mrs. Larry W. Hill, Irving, Texas

DEVILED HAMBURGER TOASTIES

1 lb. ground beef	1 tsp. salt
1/3 c. chili sauce	1 1/2 tsp. Worcestershire sauce
1 1/2 tsp. horseradish	Dash of pepper
1 1/2 tsp. prepared mustard	8 slices bread
1 tsp. minced onion	

Combine all the ingredients except the bread and mix well. Toast bread on one side in the broiler, then spread untoasted side with beef mixture. Broil for 6 minutes or until browned. Cut each sandwich into 3 strips. 24 strips.

Mrs. Soila Diaz, Cross City, Florida

HAMBURGER WHEELS

1/4 lb. hamburger	Garlic salt to taste
1 tbsp. chopped onion	1/4 c. milk
Salt and pepper to taste	1 can refrigerator biscuits

Combine the hamburger, onion, salt, pepper, garlic salt and milk and mix well. Flatten each biscuit into a 2 x 4-inch rectangle, then spread 1 tablespoon hamburger mixture evenly over each rectangle. Roll up and cut into 4 pieces. Place on greased baking sheet. Bake at 400 degrees for 15 minutes. Serve warm. 40 appetizers.

Joan D. Diener, Richmond, Virginia

SPICY MEAT-FILLED PASTRIES

1 lge. onion, finely chopped	1 1/2 tsp. salt
1 tbsp. cooking oil	2 tsp. sugar
1/2 lb. ground round steak	1 tbsp. vinegar
1 tbsp. crushed peanuts	1 c. flour
1 tbsp. raisins	1 tsp. baking powder
2 tbsp. green peas	4 tsp. shortening
1/2 tsp. ginger	3 tbsp. hot water
1/2 tsp. turmeric	

Fry the onion in oil until light brown, then add the ground steak, peanuts, raisins, green peas, ginger, turmeric and 1 teaspoon salt. Cook until beef is well browned. Add 1/2 cup water and simmer until dry and peas are cooked. Add the sugar and vinegar, mixing well. Let stand until cool. Mix the flour, remaining salt and baking powder together, then cut in shortening. Add the hot water and knead well. Shape into ball, then divide into 8 parts. Roll each part into a thin circle, then cut into halves. Place filling on each half and fold into triangular shape, pressing edges to seal. Fry in hot deep fat until golden brown. Serve hot.

Mrs. D. N. Contractor, Laurel, Maryland

PUFFS WITH BEEF

1 c. water	1 c. cooked, ground or dried beef
1/2 c. butter	1/4 c. chopped pickles
1 c. flour	1 tbsp. catsup
1 pkg. dry onion soup mix	Hot sauce to taste
4 eggs	Salad dressing

Combine the water and butter and bring to a boil. Blend in the flour, stirring constantly until mixture leaves side of pan and forms a ball. Remove from heat. Shake soup mix through a sieve over flour mixture. Beat eggs into flour mixture, one at a time, beating until smooth after each addition. Drop by 1/2 teaspoonfuls onto ungreased baking sheet. Bake at 400 degrees for 12 to 15 minutes or until dry, then cool. Combine the beef, pickles, catsup, hot sauce and enough salad dressing to moisten. Cut open puffs, then fill with beef mixture. 24 servings.

Mrs. Ethel Burns, Daytona Beach, Florida

MIDGIEBURGERS

1/2 lb. ground beef	1/4 tsp. pepper
1 egg	1 sm. onion, minced
1 tsp. salt	Bread slices, crusts trimmed
1/2 clove of garlic, minced	Catsup

Combine all ingredients except bread and catsup and mix well. Shape into small balls. Cut each slice of bread into 4 squares and place 1 meatball on each square, then press down to flatten ball. Press small hole in center of beef mixture and fill with catsup. Broil for several minutes or until firm. Serve hot.

Mrs. Della Rhodes, Williamsburg, Kentucky

EMPANADITAS

1/2 lb. ground beef	Dash of hot sauce
1/2 green pepper, chopped	1/4 tsp. steak sauce
1 onion, chopped	1 c. white cornmeal
1 8-oz. can tomato sauce	1 c. flour
1/4 tsp. garlic powder	1/2 tsp. baking powder
1 1/4 tsp. salt	1 c. lukewarm water

Combine beef, green pepper and onion in heavy skillet and cook until partially done. Add tomato sauce, garlic powder, 1 teaspoon salt, hot sauce and steak sauce, then simmer for 25 minutes. Sift the cornmeal, flour, baking powder and remaining salt together, then add lukewarm water slowly to form soft dough, stirring until well blended. Divide dough into 12 patties and flatten between sheets of waxed paper. Place 2 teaspoons of the beef mixture on each patty, then fold diagonally and seal. Brown in hot fat, turning once. Serve hot.

Mrs. William H. Fleetwood, Cape Charles, Virginia

PRESIDIO EMPANADAS

2 boxes pie crust mix
3 med. onions, minced
2 ripe tomatoes, finely chopped
2 green peppers, minced
2 cloves of garlic, mashed
1 can peeled green chilies, minced
Salad oil

1 lb. ground beef
2 tbsp. flour
2 tbsp. capers
1 tsp. sugar
Salt to taste
Chili powder to taste
Sliced stuffed olives

Prepare the pie crust mix according to package directions and chill. Saute the onions, tomatoes, green peppers, garlic and chilies in small amount oil. Stir in the beef and cook until lightly browned. Add flour, capers, sugar, salt and chili powder, then cook for 15 minutes longer. Chill. Divide the pastry into small portions, then roll out thinly and cut into 2 1/2-inch rounds. Place 1 teaspoon filling on each round, topping with an olive slice. Dampen the edges and fold over, pressing together with fork tines. Bake at 425 to 450 degrees or fry in deep fat for 15 minutes or until done. 100 appetizers.

Mrs. Elaine Cooper, Pensacola, Florida

CHILIAN EMPANADAS

1 lb. ground beef
4 white onions, minced
2 green peppers, minced
4 green chili peppers, minced
1 tbsp. oil
Salt and pepper to taste
3 hard-cooked eggs, chopped

15 chopped olives
Paprika to taste
Cayenne pepper to taste
Worcestershire sauce to taste
Hot sauce to taste
3 boxes pie crust mix

Combine beef, onions, peppers and chilies in oil in a heavy skillet and cook until onions are tender. Season with salt and pepper. Cool slightly, then add the eggs and olives and season with paprika, cayenne pepper, Worcestershire sauce and hot sauce. Chill overnight. Prepare the pastry according to package directions, then roll out dough thin. Cut in 3-inch rounds and place 1 heaping teaspoon filling on each round. Fold over and pinch together at edges with a fork. Place on baking sheet. Bake at 450 degrees for 20 minutes or until brown. These may be frozen but do not thaw before baking. 90 servings.

Mrs. Miles R. League, Tucson, Arizona

FRIED EMPANADAS

1 c. flour
1 1/2 tsp. salt
1 tsp. baking powder
2 tbsp. shortening
1/3 c. milk
1 lb. ground beef

2 tbsp. chopped onion
1 tbsp. shortening
1/4 tsp. pepper
3 tbsp. tomato paste
1 tbsp. chili powder

Combine the flour, 1/2 teaspoon salt, baking powder, shortening and milk, mixing well. Roll out very thin and cut with large biscuit cutter. Brown the beef and onion in shortening, then add the pepper, remaining salt, tomato paste and chili powder. Simmer for 15 minutes. Place small amount of beef mixture on each pastry round. Fold over and press edge with fork. Fry in deep fat at 375 degrees until brown. 50 appetizers.

Mrs. Patsy Blake, Rome, Georgia

PIROSHKI

1 c. sour cream	3/4 tsp. monosodium glutamate
1/2 c. melted butter	3/4 tsp. salt
1/2 tsp. sugar	1/8 tsp. pepper
2 eggs, separated	2 tbsp. butter or margarine
2 c. sifted all-purpose flour	1 tsp. minced onion
1 lb. ground beef	

Beat a small amount of the sour cream into the melted butter, then blend in the remaining sour cream. Stir in sugar and egg yolks, then blend in the flour gradually. Place in small, lightly floured bowl and sprinkle top of pastry with small amount of additional flour. Cover lightly with waxed paper and chill overnight. Break up the beef with a fork in a mixing bowl. Sprinkle monosodium glutamate, salt and pepper over beef and toss lightly to distribute seasonings. Melt the butter in a skillet, then add the onion and beef. Cook, breaking up with a fork, until lightly browned. Roll chilled dough to 1/16-inch thickness on lightly floured board or pastry cloth. Cut out dough with a 3-inch round cookie cutter. Brush inside edge of each round with egg white, then fill each with 1 teaspoon of the beef mixture. Bring opposite sides of the rounds together and seal tightly with fingers. Place on ungreased cookie sheets, sealed side down. Brush tops lightly with egg white. Bake at 400 degrees for 20 minutes or until lightly browned. 3 dozen.

Photograph for this recipe on page 9.

CHAFING DISH MEATBALLS

2 lb. ground beef	1 bottle chili sauce
1 egg, slightly beaten	1/2 lge. jar grape jelly
1 lge. white onion, grated	Juice of 1 lemon
Salt to taste	

Place the ground beef, egg, onion and salt in a bowl and mix well. Shape into marble-sized balls. Combine remaining ingredients in a saucepan and add the meatballs. Simmer until meatballs are done. Place in a chafing dish to serve. 35 servings.

Mrs. Charles A. Haden, Nashville, Tennessee

Party Meatballs (below)

PARTY MEATBALLS

1 lb. ground lean beef	1/4 c. catsup or chili sauce
1/2 c. corn flake crumbs	1 tbsp. Worcestershire sauce
1/2 c. evaporated milk	1 tsp. salt
1/4 c. finely cut onion	1 tsp. pepper

Combine all the ingredients in a 2-quart bowl and mix well. Shape into 36 small meatballs, using about 1 teaspoon for each. Place in 13 x 9 x 2-inch pan. Bake in a 400-degree oven for 12 to 15 minutes or until brown.

Dunky Sauce

1 8-oz. can tomato sauce	2 tbsp. water
1/2 c. catsup	2 tbsp. Worcestershire sauce
2 tbsp. brown sugar	1 tbsp. vinegar
2 tbsp. finely cut onion	Dash of pepper
2 tbsp. pickle relish, drained	

Combine all ingredients in a 2-quart saucepan and mix well. Cook until heated through, then serve with meatballs.

SAVORY MEATBALLS

1 tsp. monosodium glutamate	1 egg
1 tsp. salt	1/2 c. dry bread crumbs
1/8 tsp. pepper	1/4 c. grated Parmesan cheese
1 lb. ground beef	1 tbsp. chopped onion

1/4 tsp. oregano or basil
Dash of nutmeg
Dash of dry mustard

2 tbsp. butter or margarine
1/4 c. chili sauce

Sprinkle the monosodium glutamate, salt and pepper on the ground beef in a mixing bowl. Add the remaining ingredients except the butter and chili sauce and mix thoroughly. Moisten hands with water and shape the beef mixture into small balls, about 1 inch in diameter. Melt the butter in a skillet and add several meatballs at a time, then cook until lightly browned on all sides, moving pan constantly. Return all the meatballs to skillet and heat. May flame with brandy, if desired. Remove the meatballs to a platter or chafing dish. Add the chili sauce to skillet and heat, scraping in any bits of meat remaining in pan. Serve as a dip for the meatballs. 3 dozen meatballs.

Photograph for this recipe on page 9.

BASIL MEATBALLS

4 tbsp. cream
3 tbsp. water
1/4 c. fine rusk crumbs
1 tsp. basil
1/4 tsp. cayenne pepper

1 tsp. salt
3/4 lb. ground beef
1/4 lb. ground pork
2 tbsp. grated onion
Butter or margarine

Combine the cream and water, then add the crumbs. Combine the remaining ingredients except the butter and mix well, then add the rusk mixture. Mix until smooth. Shape into balls, then brown in a small amount of butter. Serve hot. May be served with potatoes or spaghetti.

Photograph for this recipe on page 14.

CHINESE MEATBALLS

1 lb. ground beef
1/2 c. fine bread crumbs
Milk
1 egg, beaten
2 tbsp. flour
Salt and pepper to taste
1/2 c. cooking oil
1 can pineapple chunks

1 c. chicken broth or bouillon
2 lge. green peppers, cut in
   1-in. squares
3 tbsp. cornstarch
1 tbsp. soy sauce
1/2 tsp. monosodium glutamate
1/2 c. brown sugar

Combine the beef and crumbs with enough milk to hold together, then shape into small balls. Combine the egg, flour, salt and pepper and mix until smooth. Heat the oil in a large skillet. Dip the meatballs into the egg mixture, then fry until brown on all sides. Remove meatballs and keep warm. Drain the pineapple, reserving 1/2 cup juice. Drain all but 1 teaspoon fat from the skillet and add the broth, green peppers and pineapple chunks. Cover and cook over medium heat for 10 minutes. Blend reserved pineapple juice with all the remaining ingredients and stir into the skillet. Cook, stirring constantly, until thick. Return meatballs to sauce and heat.

Mrs. Alice Grant, Martin, Tennessee

COCKTAIL MEATBALLS IN WINE

1 lb. ground beef	3 eggs, beaten
1/2 lb. ground pork	1/2 c. flour
1/4 c. minced onion	Cooking oil
1/2 c. bread crumbs	2 c. Chablis or sauterne
4 tbsp. capers	2 tsp. grated orange rind
Salt and pepper to taste	3 tbsp. tomato paste
1 tsp. thyme	

Combine the meats, onion, bread crumbs, seasonings and eggs and mix well. Shape into small meatballs, then roll in flour. Brown well in hot oil. Mix the Chablis, orange rind and tomato paste in a saucepan and bring to a boil. Add the meatballs and simmer for 1 hour and 30 minutes. Serve in a chafing dish.

Mrs. Dorothy Connelly, Corpus Christi, Texas

APPETIZER CHEESE MEATBALLS

1 1/2 lb. ground beef	1/8 tsp. pepper
1 3-oz. package Roquefort	1/4 c. butter
cheese, crumbled	1/2 c. Burgundy cooking wine
3/4 tsp. salt	or beef bouillon

Combine the beef, cheese, salt and pepper and mix well. Shape into balls, using 1 heaping teaspoon for each. Brown the meatballs in the butter, turning to brown all sides. Add the wine and cover. Cook slowly for 3 to 5 minutes. 6 dozen meatballs.

Appetizer Cheese Meatballs (above)

GROUND CHUCK FONDUE

1 1/2 lb. ground chuck	1/2 c. catsup
1 sm. onion, minced	2 tbsp. sweet relish
1 tsp. monosodium glutamate	1 c. sour cream
1 tsp. salt	2 tsp. horseradish
1/4 tsp. pepper	2 tbsp. pickled red cabbage
2 tbsp. prepared mustard	1 qt. salad oil
1/2 c. mayonnaise	

Combine the ground chuck, onion, monosodium glutamate, salt and pepper in a bowl and mix well. Shape into 1-inch meatballs. Arrange on a cookie sheet covered with waxed paper and cover meatballs with a sheet of waxed paper. Refrigerate until chilled. Mix the mustard and mayonnaise in a small serving bowl. Blend the catsup with relish in another bowl. Blend 1/2 cup sour cream with horseradish in a bowl and blend the pickled cabbage with remaining sour cream in a bowl. Cover each bowl with plastic wrap and refrigerate until chilled. Heat the salad oil in a metal fondue pot over medium heat until very hot and place on stand over fondue burner. Place meatballs on fondue forks and cook in oil for about 2 minutes or to desired doneness. Serve with chilled sauces.

Mrs. A. C. James, Springfield, Louisiana

HOPPED MEATBALLS

3 lb. ground beef	1/4 c. water
1 lge. onion, grated	1 14-oz. bottle catsup
Salt and pepper to taste	1 12-oz. can beer
Garlic powder to taste	

Combine the beef, onion, salt, pepper and garlic powder and mix well. Shape into bite-sized meatballs. Combine the remaining ingredients in a saucepan and bring to a boil, then drop the meatballs carefully into sauce. Simmer for 1 hour. Serve in sauce in a chafing dish. May be prepared in advance. 50-55 meatballs.

Mrs. Sylvia Martin, Virginia Beach, Virginia

OLIVE MEATBALLS

1/2 lb. ground beef	1/2 tsp. garlic salt
1 egg	1/2 tsp. onion salt
1/2 c. dry bread crumbs	24 sm. stuffed olives
1/3 c. lemon-lime carbonated drink	

Combine all the ingredients except the olives and mix well. Measure by table-spoons and flatten, then place an olive in center and mold meat mixture around olive. Broil, 2 inches from heat, for 6 to 8 minutes, turning once. Serve hot with toothpick in each meatball. 24 meatballs.

Mrs. Joseph Cannon, Springfield, West Virginia

COCKTAIL MEATBALLS TO FREEZE

2 lb. ground beef	Salt and pepper to taste
1 sm. onion, grated	1 bottle chili sauce
1 clove of garlic, crushed	Juice of 1 lemon
1/2 c. corn flakes, crushed	1 6-oz. glass grape jelly
2 eggs, beaten	

Combine the ground beef, onion, garlic, corn flakes, eggs, salt and pepper and mix well. Shape into walnut-sized balls. Combine the remaining ingredients in a heavy skillet and simmer for 5 minutes. Place meatballs in the sauce and cook slowly for 1 hour. Cool. Refrigerate until fat hardens, then skim off and discard fat. Pour into freezer containers and freeze. Reheat to serve. 65 servings.

Mrs. Dora Dickinson, Winter Haven, Florida

MEATBALLS IN BURGUNDY

1 lb. ground beef	1/2 tsp. savory
1 c. quick oats	1/2 onion, grated
1/4 c. evaporated milk	Shortening
1 egg, beaten	1 1/2 tbsp. flour
1 tsp. salt	1 can beef consomme
1/2 tsp. pepper	1/2 c. Burgundy
1/2 tsp. thyme	

Combine the beef, oats, milk, egg, salt, pepper, thyme, savory and onion and mix well. Shape into small balls and brown in a small amount of shortening. Drain on paper towels. Brown the flour in a small amount of the drippings, then stir in the consomme and Burgundy and simmer until thickened. Pour over meatballs in a chafing dish and simmer until served. 20 servings.

Mrs. Thelma Wilson, Oxford, Mississippi

BITE-SIZED PIZZA SNACKS

1 lb. ground beef	Salt and pepper to taste
1 sm. can tomato paste	2 loaves party rye bread
1 sm. can tomato sauce	Mozzarella cheese slices
1 tsp. oregano	Thin tomato slices
1/4 tsp. garlic powder	Sliced mushrooms

Combine the beef, paste, sauce, oregano, garlic powder, salt and pepper and mix well. Spread on the bread slices, then top with the cheese, tomato and mushroom slices. Place on an ungreased cookie sheet. Bake at 350 degrees on lower shelf of oven for 10 to 15 minutes.

Mrs. Fran Boyles, Memphis, Tennessee

MINIATURE ITALIAN PIZZAS

1 can tomato sauce	1/2 tsp. oregano
1/4 tsp. garlic salt	1/2 tsp. pepper

1/4 tsp. dry mustard
1 tsp. chili powder
1/4 c. minced onion
1 can refrigerator biscuits

Cooked ground beef
Chopped olives
Chopped mushrooms
Grated or sliced cheese

Combine the tomato sauce, garlic salt, oregano, pepper, mustard, chili powder and onion in a saucepan and bring to a boil. Roll out biscuits for individual pizzas. Spread with the ground beef and sprinkle with the olives, mushrooms and cheese. Cover with the sauce. Place on baking sheet. Bake at 400 degrees for 15 to 20 minutes or until edges are brown. 10 servings.

Mrs. Barbara H. Thompson, Tom Bean, Texas

SLOPPY JOE PIZZA

1 13 3/4-oz. package hot
   roll mix
1 lb. ground beef
1 tbsp. prepared mustard
1 egg
1/2 tsp. salt
1 6-oz. can tomato paste

1 1 1/2-oz. envelope seasoning
   mix for Sloppy Joes
1/2 c. water
Grated Parmesan cheese
Leaf oregano to taste
6 oz. mozzarella cheese, sliced

Prepare the hot roll mix for pizza dough according to package directions, using 1 cup warm water. Set aside. Mix the beef, mustard, egg and salt together. Blend the tomato paste, seasoning mix and water together in a small bowl. Pat or roll pizza dough to fit a greased 15 x 10 1/2-inch jelly roll pan. Spread top of dough with beef mixture, then with the tomato paste mixture. Sprinkle with Parmesan cheese and oregano. Bake in a 450-degree oven for 20 minutes. Remove from oven and cut into 12 squares. Place a slice of mozzarella cheese on each square and garnish with sliced stuffed olives, if desired. Return to oven for about 5 minutes or until cheese melts. 12 servings.

Sloppy Joe Pizza (above)

HOT MEXICAN SALAD

1 1/2 lb. hamburger	1 lb. Velveeta cheese, cubed
1 c. chopped green pepper	1 can stewed tomatoes with green
1 c. chopped celery	pepper and onion
1 1/2 c. chopped onion	1 head lettuce, shredded
3 garlic buds, crushed	1 lge. tomato, cubed
1 tbsp. chili powder	1 lge. bag corn chips
Salt to taste	

Combine the first 7 ingredients in frypan and saute until lightly browned. Melt the cheese in a double boiler and stir in the tomatoes. Combine the lettuce and tomato, then toss with the hamburger mixture. Add the corn chips and pour the cheese mixture over all. Serve at once. 4 servings.

Mrs. Harriet Stone, Austin, Texas

GROUND BEEF SURPRISE

1 lb. ground beef	1/2 c. finely chopped celery
1/4 c. pickle relish	Mayonnaise
2 tbsp. minced onion	

Saute the ground beef until lightly browned, stirring frequently, then drain well. Mix in the relish, onion and celery. Blend in enough mayonnaise to moisten and hold mixture together, then chill. Serve in lettuce cups. 6-8 servings.

Mrs. Elinor Hall, Oxford, Mississippi

LUNCHEON SALAD

1 lb. ground beef	1 can mushroom soup
1 sm. onion, chopped	1 head lettuce, chopped
1/2 green pepper, chopped	1/2 pkg. corn chips
1 clove of garlic, minced	Tomato wedges
1/2 lb. Velveeta cheese, cubed	

Combine the beef, onion, green pepper and garlic in a skillet and lightly brown. Combine the cheese and soup in top of double boiler and cook, stirring, until cheese is melted. Place the lettuce in a large salad bowl and sprinkle the corn chips over top. Spread the hot beef mixture over chips. Garnish with tomatoes. Pour hot cheese mixture over top and toss. 8 servings.

Mrs. Melanie Thompson, Gadsden, Alabama

SUPREME CHUCK SALAD

1 lb. finely ground chuck	1 1/2 c. chopped lettuce
3 c. water	1 sm. tomato, diced
1 tsp. salt	1/4 c. salad dressing
1/2 tsp. pepper	1/2 c. chopped drained mushrooms
1 sm. onion, finely chopped	

Place the ground chuck, water, salt and pepper in a saucepan and simmer until chuck is tender. Drain and place in a salad bowl. Add the onion, lettuce and tomato. Add the salad dressing and mushrooms and mix well. 8 servings.

Mrs. W. W. Thorne, Jewett, Texas

HOT BEEF SALAD

1/2 head lettuce, chopped	1 8-oz. can tomato sauce
1 tomato, diced	2 tbsp. chili powder
1 onion, chopped	Salt and pepper to taste
1 lb. ground beef	1 med. package corn chips

Combine the lettuce, tomato and onion. Saute the ground beef until lightly browned, then add the tomato sauce, chili powder, salt and pepper. Cook until flavors are blended. Pour beef mixture over salad and toss. Add the corn chips and toss lightly. Serve immediately. 6 servings.

Mrs. Allen Daggett, Houston, Texas

SLOPPY JOE ON THE HALF SHELL

1 lb. lean ground beef	1 8-oz. can tomato sauce
1 1 1/2-oz. package Sloppy	3 California avocados, halved
Joe seasoning mix	and peeled
1 c. water	6 onion rings

Brown the ground beef in a skillet, then drain off the fat. Add the seasoning mix, water and tomato sauce, then simmer for 10 minutes, stirring occasionally. Spoon mixture into avocado half shells. Top with onions. Serve with toasted buns. 6 servings.

Sloppy Joe on the Half Shell (above)

Chili and Chips (page 34)

soups & stews

Is there a family that doesn't respond with warm compliments when homemade soups and stews are put before them? *Southern Living* homemakers don't think so — and they are past masters at transforming meat, vegetables, seasonings, and water into masterpieces of the culinary art.

In the following section, the best of their ground beef soup and stew recipes are shared with you. Southern women enjoy using ground beef in these recipes because it not only mixes and matches with the flavor of many favorite recipe ingredients, but it takes less cooking time than tougher soup and stew meat.

Chili is one of the best known ground beef soups. Discover why when you taste the hot and hearty goodness of Western Chili (the recipe is included in this section). Then introduce your family to Hamburger French Onion Soup — it's a flavorful meal in a bowl . . . Hamburger Skillet Stew . . . or any one of the great ground beef soup and stew recipes from the pages that follow. Their ease of preparation and delicious flavors will dazzle you!

Shouldn't you begin to explore this section now — and introduce your family to a great ground beef soup or stew — tonight? You'll be so glad you did, and so will they!

WESTERN CHILI

1 lb. chili beans	1 tsp. paprika
1 tbsp. fat	Salt to taste
1 lb. ground beef	1/4 tsp. pepper
2 sm. onions, chopped	1 1/2 tsp. chili powder
2 c. tomato puree	1 2-in. red pepper (opt.)

Wash the beans, then soak overnight in enough water to cover. Drain and place in large saucepan, then cover with salted water. Cook slowly until tender. Heat fat in large skillet and add the beef and onions, then cook until brown, stirring with a fork. Add the tomato puree and the beef mixture to the beans and mix well. Stir in the seasonings and cover, then simmer for about 30 minutes.

Mrs. Elmer Sharpton, Logan, Alabama

AROMATIC CHILI CON CARNE

1 med. onion, chopped	1 8-oz. can tomato sauce
1 clove of garlic, minced	2 tbsp. flour
1/4 lb. butter	2 tsp. salt
1 1/2 lb. ground beef	1 tbsp. chili powder
2 1/2 c. canned kidney beans	2 tbsp. angostura aromatic
1 16-oz. can tomatoes	bitters

Saute the onion and garlic in butter, then add the beef and brown. Place in a large pan, then add the remaining ingredients and mix well. Simmer for 30 minutes, stirring occasionally, and adding water or additional tomato sauce if needed. 6 servings.

Aromatic Chili Con Carne (above)

Hot Tomatorie Chili (below)

HOT TOMATORIE CHILI

6 tbsp. butter or salad oil
4 med. onions, sliced
2 med. green peppers, cut in
strips
1 c. coarsely cut celery
3 lb. ground beef
3 20-oz. cans tomatoes

2 6-oz. cans tomato paste
1 tbsp. salt
2 tsp. monosodium glutamate
1 tsp. hot sauce
2 tbsp. chili powder
3 20-oz. cans kidney beans

Melt the butter in a Dutch oven, then add the onions, green peppers and celery and cook until onion is tender, but not brown. Add the ground beef and cook until beef loses red color, breaking up with a fork. Add the tomatoes, tomato paste, salt, monosodium glutamate, hot sauce and chili powder. Cover and simmer for 45 minutes. Add the kidney beans and simmer for 20 minutes longer. Serve with crisp, salted crackers. 12 servings.

CHILI PRONTO

1 lb. ground beef
1 c. chopped onion
1 No. 2 can red kidney beans
1 No. 2 can tomatoes
2 c. water

2 tsp. chili powder
2 tsp. salt
1 tsp. paprika
Garlic salt to taste

Saute the ground beef and onion in a small amount of fat until brown. Add the remaining ingredients and heat thoroughly.

Mrs. Ralph Chapman, Lewisburg, Tennessee

CHILI AND CHIPS

.2 15 1/2-oz. cans chili
   with beans
1 c. crumbled tortilla chips

1 4-oz. package shredded
   Cheddar cheese

Place the chili in a saucepan and simmer until heated through. Stir in the tortilla chips and cheese and heat for 5 minutes longer. Serve in bowls with whole tortilla chips.

Photograph for this recipe on page 30.

CHEESE AND BEEF SOUP

1 lb. ground beef
1/2 c. finely chopped celery
1/4 c. chopped onion
2 tbsp. chopped green pepper
3 tbsp. flour

1/2 tsp. salt
4 c. milk
1 tbsp. beef-flavored gravy base
1 c. shredded sharp Cheddar cheese

Brown the ground beef in a large saucepan and add the celery, onion, and green pepper. Cook until the vegetables are tender. Blend in the flour and salt, then stir in the milk and gravy base slowly and simmer, stirring, until thickened. Add the cheese and cook and stir just until the cheese melts. 4-6 servings.

Mrs. Martha Meriwether, Montgomery, Alabama

BEEF SOUP

1 1/2 to 2 lb. ground beef
1 8-oz. can tomato sauce
1 1-lb. 1-oz. can garden peas
1 pkg. frozen corn
3 carrots, sliced

1 lge. onion, sliced
Salt to taste
Pepper to taste
1 tbsp. sugar
4 med. potatoes, cubed

Combine all the ingredients except the potatoes in a large pot. Add water to cover and cook for 1 hour. Add the potatoes and cook for 30 minutes longer, adding water if needed.

Mrs. J. W. Williford, Rebecca, Georgia

BEEF-BARLEY SOUP

2 lb. ground beef
1 stick margarine
4 qt. water
1 c. diced carrots
3 c. diced celery

1 lge. can tomatoes
1/2 c. pearl barley
2 tsp. salt
3 tsp. pepper
2 lge. onions, chopped

Brown the beef in margarine in a heavy kettle. Add the remaining ingredients and simmer for 2 hours, stirring occasionally.

Mrs. Lillian Herman, Bay City, Texas

CREAMED HAMBURGER SOUP

1/2 c. chopped onion	1/2 tsp. salt
1/4 c. chopped green pepper	1/4 tsp. pepper
1 tbsp. cooking oil	1/2 tsp. savory salt
1/2 lb. ground beef	1/2 c. diced potatoes
1 c. tomato juice	2 tbsp. flour
1/2 c. sliced carrots	2 c. milk

Saute the onion and green pepper in oil in skillet till tender but not brown. Add the beef and cook until brown. Stir in tomato juice, carrots and seasonings. Cover and cook till carrots are almost tender. Add the potatoes and simmer until vegetables are done. Blend the flour and a small amount of milk to smooth paste, then add the remaining milk gradually. Stir the milk mixture into soup slowly. Bring to a boil and cook for 2 to 3 minutes longer. 4 servings.

Mrs. Lenore Bergmann, Richmond, Virginia

GOULASH

2 lb. ground beef	1 lge. can tomato juice
1 lge. onion, chopped	2 tsp. salt
2 c. cooked spaghetti	1 tsp. chili powder
1 can kidney beans	1/2 tsp. pepper
1 can tomato paste	

Brown the ground beef and onion in a heavy skillet. Mix remaining ingredients in a large kettle and add the beef mixture. Simmer for about 1 hour and 30 minutes, adding water or additional tomato juice, if needed.

Ann Elsie Schmetzer, Madisonville, Kentucky

GUMBO SOUP

1 1/2 lb. ground chuck	1 c. butter beans
4 slices bacon, chopped	1 tbsp. chopped bell pepper
3/4 c. chopped onion	1 No. 2 can tomatoes
1 tsp. salt	1 c. whole kernel corn
1/2 tsp. pepper	2 c. sliced okra
3 c. water	1 bay leaf
1 c. purple hull or field peas	1 tbsp. gumbo file

Cook the ground chuck, bacon, onion, salt and pepper in a large, heavy kettle until brown, stirring frequently. Add the water and bring to a boil. Add the peas, butter beans and bell pepper and cook until vegetables are done, adding water, if needed. Add the tomatoes, corn, okra and bay leaf and cook for 15 minutes longer. Remove the bay leaf and stir in the gumbo file. May be served over rice. 6-8 servings.

Mrs. Rose Girlinghouse, Pineville, Louisiana

Beef-Potato Soup (below)

BEEF-POTATO SOUP

1 5 5/8-oz. package scalloped potatoes	1 10-oz. package frozen peas and carrots
7 c. water	1/4 c. instant minced onion
2 10-oz. cans beef broth	1 1/4 tsp. salt
2 6-oz. cans tomato paste	1 lb. ground beef
1 c. diced celery	

Combine all the ingredients except the beef in a 6-quart stew pot, then bring to a boil over moderate heat. Drop heaping teaspoonfuls of beef into the boiling mixture. Bring to a boil again, then reduce the heat and cover. Simmer for 30 to 40 minutes or until vegetables are tender. 8-10 servings.

HAMBURGER MINESTRONE

1 lb. ground beef	1 sm. bay leaf
1 c. chopped onions	1/2 tsp. thyme
1 c. cubed potatoes	1/4 tsp. basil
1 c. sliced carrots	1 tbsp. salt
1/2 c. diced celery	1/8 tsp. pepper
1 c. shredded cabbage	6 c. water
1 No. 2 can tomatoes	Grated Parmesan cheese
1/4 c. rice	

Cook the beef and onions in a kettle until brown. Add the potatoes and bring to a boil. Add remaining ingredients except cheese and cover. Simmer for 1 hour, stirring occasionally. Sprinkle with cheese just before serving. 6 servings.

Mrs. Philip Booker, Austin, Texas

CONSOMME MADRILENE

4 tomatoes	2 1/2 pt. beef stock
1 c. minced beef	1 egg white, well beaten
Salt and pepper to taste	

Peel and slice the tomatoes and place in a saucepan. Add the beef, salt and pepper and stir well. Add the stock and egg white and stir well. Simmer for 1 hour. Strain and serve.

Mrs. Larry Hyland, Memphis, Tennessee

HAMBURGER-FRENCH ONION SOUP

1 tbsp. butter	1 can beef stock
1/2 lb. hamburger	1 c. water
10 med. onions, thinly sliced	2 beef bouillon cubes

Brown the butter in a large kettle. Add the hamburger and cook until brown, stirring frequently. Add the onions, beef stock, water and bouillon cubes and simmer for 30 minutes. Serve with squares of buttered toast and Parmesan cheese.

Mrs. Katie Black, Cunningham, Tennessee

HAMBURGER SOUP

1 lge. onion, chopped	1/3 tsp. soda
1/2 lb. hamburger	4 c. scalded milk
2 c. canned tomatoes	

Fry the onion in small amount of fat until browned. Add the hamburger and cook for 5 minutes, stirring frequently. Add tomatoes and bring to a boil. Add the soda and milk and serve at once.

Mrs. Rufus Slabauch, Grantsville, Maryland

INDIAN CORN STEW

1 med. onion, chopped	1 can tomato soup
1/3 c. chopped green pepper	2 tsp. sugar
2 tbsp. margarine	1 1/2 tsp. salt
1 lb. ground beef	1 tbsp. Worcestershire sauce
2 1/2 c. corn, cut from cob	

Cook the onion and green pepper in margarine in a large saucepan until tender. Add the beef and cook until brown. Add the corn, tomato soup, sugar, salt and Worcestershire sauce and simmer for 1 hour.

Mrs. Norman Milam, Bowling Green, Kentucky

37

HOMEMADE HAMBURGER SOUP

1/2 c. butter	1 c. diced potatoes
1 c. chopped onions	1 1/2 tsp. salt
1 c. sliced carrots	1/8 tsp. pepper
1/2 c. chopped green pepper	1/3 c. flour
1 lb. ground beef	4 c. milk
2 c. tomato juice	

Melt the butter in a large saucepan. Add the onions, carrots and green pepper and cook until onions are tender. Add the beef and cook until brown. Stir in the tomato juice, potatoes and seasonings. Cover and cook over low heat for 20 to 25 minutes or until vegetables are tender. Mix the flour and 1 cup milk until smooth, then stir into soup mixture. Add remaining milk and bring to a boil. Serve at once.

Mrs. C. A. Davidson, Amarillo, Texas

LATVIAN MEATBALL AND POTATO SOUP

4 lge. potatoes, cut in eighths	1/4 c. milk
8 peppercorns	1 med. onion, chopped
1 bay leaf	1 egg
2 1/2 tsp. salt	1/4 tsp. pepper
8 c. water	1 lb. hamburger
2 slices bread, crumbled	1/2 c. flour

Place the potatoes, peppercorns, bay leaf, 1 teaspoon salt and water in a large kettle and bring to a boil. Reduce heat and simmer for about 30 minutes or until potatoes are almost done. Mix the bread, milk, onion, egg, remaining salt, pepper and hamburger and shape into small balls. Roll in flour, then drop into potato mixture. Simmer for about 20 minutes or until meatballs are tender. 8-10 servings.

Mrs. Doris Yeager, Cameron, Oklahoma

MEATBALL SOUP

1 lb. ground beef	Dash of pepper
Pinch of oregano	1/4 c. bread crumbs
1 egg	2 cans chicken broth
1 tsp. parsley flakes	1 c. fine egg noodles
1/2 tsp. salt	

Mix the ground beef, oregano, egg, parsley flakes, salt, pepper and bread crumbs and shape into meatballs about 1/2 inch in diameter. Pour the broth into a saucepan and bring to a boil. Add the meatballs and simmer for about 20 minutes. Add the noodles and cook for about 15 minutes or until noodles are tender. 4 servings.

Mrs. Frank Wilson, Anderson, South Carolina

CONSOMME AND MEATBALL SOUP

1 lb. ground beef
3/4 tsp. salt
3/4 tsp. chili powder
1 sm. onion, grated
1 c. fine bread crumbs
1/2 c. pine nuts

1 egg, slightly beaten
2 cans beef consomme
2 soup cans water
1 bay leaf
1/4 c. dry sherry

Mix the ground beef, salt, chili powder, onion, bread crumbs, pine nuts and egg and shape into meatballs about 1 inch in diameter. Pour the consomme and water into a saucepan and add the bay leaf. Bring to a boil. Add the meatballs, several at a time. Reduce heat and cover. Simmer for 30 minutes. Remove the bay leaf and stir in the sherry just before serving. 4-6 servings.

Mrs. M. A. Meadows, Alexandria, Virginia

QUICK VEGETABLE SOUP

1 lb. ground beef
1 c. chopped onion
2 c. chopped cabbage
1 No. 2 can mixed vegetables
1 No. 2 1/2 can tomatoes

2 1/2 tsp. salt
1/4 tsp. pepper
1/2 tsp. garlic powder
3 c. water
1 c. shell macaroni

Brown the beef in a kettle over medium heat. Add remaining ingredients except macaroni and bring to a boil. Add the macaroni and cover. Simmer for 15 minutes. 5-8 servings.

Mrs. Wes Yates, Dover, Delaware

HAMBURGER SKILLET STEW

1 lb. ground beef
1/4 c. fine bread crumbs
1/4 c. chopped onion
1 egg
2 1/2 tsp. salt
1/4 tsp. pepper
1 tbsp. Worcestershire sauce
2 8-oz. cans tomato sauce

2 tbsp. vegetable oil
4 carrots, sliced
1 pkg. frozen green beans
1 lge. onion, quartered
2 potatoes, quartered
1 c. water
1 tbsp. flour

Combine the beef, bread crumbs, onion, egg, 1 1/2 teaspoons salt, pepper, Worcestershire sauce and 1/2 cup tomato sauce and shape into 16 balls. Brown in the oil in a skillet. Add the vegetables, water, remaining salt and remaining tomato sauce and mix well. Bring to a boil and cover. Reduce heat and simmer for 1 hour, stirring occasionally. Remove 1/2 cup liquid and mix with flour. Stir into stew gradually and cook over low heat until thickened. 4 servings.

Mrs. Kim White, Kuttawa, Kentucky

CALIFORNIA BEEF AND SUNSHINE STEW

1 eggplant, cubed
4 onions, peeled and quartered
2 cloves of garlic, minced
1/4 c. cooking oil
1   10 1/2-oz. can beef broth
1/2 tsp. thyme
4 zucchini, cut into 1/2-in.
    slices

5 tomatoes, peeled and
    quartered
2 green peppers, cut into
    strips
1 tsp. salt
1/4 tsp. pepper
Beef Balls

Cook the eggplant, onions and garlic in oil until partially done, stirring gently to prevent sticking. Add the broth and thyme. Cover and simmer for 10 minutes. Add the zucchini and cook for 5 minutes longer. Add the tomatoes and green peppers, then sprinkle with salt and pepper. Top with the browned Beef Balls. Cover and cook for 10 minutes. Serve at once.

Beef Balls

1/2 c. finely chopped onion
1 tbsp. cooking oil
1 egg, lightly beaten
1 c. soft bread crumbs
1/2 c. milk

1 1/2 tsp. salt
1/2 tsp. monosodium glutamate
1/4 tsp. pepper
1 1/2 lb. ground beef chuck

Saute the onion in oil until transparent. Combine the egg, crumbs, milk, salt, monosodium glutamate and pepper, mixing well. Add the onion and beef, beating with fork until well blended. Shape into 24 small balls and place on a lightly oiled pan. Bake in a 400-degree oven for 10 to 15 minutes. 8 servings.

Photograph for this recipe on page 5.

HAMBURGER STEW

1 lb. hamburger
1 lge. green pepper, diced
2 sm. onions, chopped
1/4 c. flour
2 1/2 c. water

1 1/2 tsp. salt
1/4 tsp. marjoram
4 sm. carrots, diced
2 med. potatoes, diced

Brown the hamburger in a saucepan. Add the green pepper and onions and cook until onions are transparent. Stir in the flour. Add the water, seasonings and vegetables and cook until vegetables are tender. 4 servings.

Mrs. Howard F. Smith, Greenwood, Delaware

MEATBALL STEW

2 1/2 lb. ground beef
1/2 tsp. garlic salt
1 tsp. pepper

2 eggs
2 tbsp. Worcestershire sauce
6 carrots, halved

1 c. diced celery
6 sm. onions
2 No. 303 cans whole new potatoes

1 can beef broth
1 can mushroom steak sauce

Mix the ground beef with garlic salt, pepper, eggs and Worcestershire sauce and shape into balls. Cook in a Dutch oven until brown, then drain. Place the carrots, celery and onions in a saucepan and cover with boiling water. Cook until onions are almost done, then drain. Add to meatballs. Add remaining ingredients and cover. Bake at 350 degrees until meatballs are tender. 4 servings.

Mrs. Connaola Sweeney, Belton, Texas

BEEF BALL STEW

2 lb. ground beef
2 c. water
Salt to taste
6 carrots, cubed

1 can green peas
6 potatoes, cubed
6 sm. sweet potatoes, cubed

Shape the ground beef into balls and place in a 3-quart saucepan. Add remaining ingredients and bring to a boil. Reduce heat and cover. Simmer for 30 minutes.

Zelma Hardwick, Kidder, Kentucky

MEATBALL AND VEGETABLE STEW

1 lb. ground beef
Salt and pepper to taste
1 No. 2 can cream-style corn
1 No. 2 can tomatoes
1 c. chopped potatoes

1 c. chopped carrots
1/2 c. chopped onion
1/2 c. chopped celery
1/2 c. chopped bell pepper
1/2 c. hot water

Season the ground beef with salt and pepper and shape into 8 balls. Brown in a Dutch oven, then drain. Add remaining ingredients and mix well. Bake at 325 degrees for 1 hour. 8 servings.

Mrs. W. W. McCrory, Dothan, Alabama

RANCH-STYLE STEW

1 lb. ground beef
1 med. onion, chopped
1 green pepper, diced
1 tbsp. shortening
1 1/2 c. whole kernel corn

1 No. 2 can kidney beans
1 tsp. salt
2 c. tomatoes
1 tsp. chili powder
1/2 c. water

Brown the beef, onion and green pepper in shortening in a large skillet. Add the corn, beans, salt, tomatoes, chili powder and water and simmer for 20 minutes.

June Windsor, Marlow, Oklahoma

VIP Cheeseburgers and Fries (page 48)

sandwiches

For millions of American families, ground beef means "hamburgers," those piping hot, juicy sandwiches served in their own special bun with numerous relishes and sauces. Hamburgers and other ground beef sandwiches are popular fare in the South, where virtually every community has its own special sauces or condiments which accompany the sandwich.

Explore this varied world with the recipes you'll find in the pages of this section. For a savory treat, serve Broiled Deviled Beef Sandwiches — they cook in just minutes under your broiler and are certain to bring praise from your happy family. You'll discover recipes for Hero Burgers, a ground beef variation of an all-time favorite sandwich . . . Pizzaburgers, combining two of America's favorite foods in one tomato-y rich sandwich . . . Hot Meat Loaf Sandwich, the perfect way to use leftovers.

Feature Barbecued Slawburgers or Hamburger Stroganoff Buns the next time you're looking for a quick and easy but exciting supper — the compliments you will receive will let you know that this section was made just for you!

Every recipe in these pages has been served to a family like yours, and has been acclaimed a favorite by hungry children and a husband who wants foods which please his palate. Now they're waiting here to become your family's favorites, too.

Long Burgers (below)

LONG BURGERS

1 lb. ground beef	2 oz. grated American cheese
Salt and pepper to taste	4 toasted frankfurter rolls
4 sweet gherkins, quartered	Catsup
lengthwise	Mustard

Season the ground beef with salt and pepper, then shape into 6 x 5-inch patties. Place gherkins in center of each hamburger lengthwise, then sprinkle with cheese. Roll up each burger to frankfurter shape and broil or panfry. Serve on rolls with catsup and mustard. 4 servings.

BEEF ON RYE

1 10 3/4-oz. can tomato soup	6 slices rye bread, lightly
1 lb. ground beef	toasted
1/4 c. finely chopped onion	6 slices process cheese
1/4 tsp. salt	12 thin green pepper rings
Dash of pepper	

Mix 1/3 cup of the soup, beef, onion, salt and pepper together, then spread evenly over toast, covering edges completely. Broil 3 to 4 inches from heat for 8 to 10 minutes or to desired doneness. Top with the cheese, green pepper and remaining soup, then broil until heated through and cheese is melted. 6 sandwiches.

Jeanne Day, Seaford, Delaware

BROILED DEVILED BEEF SANDWICHES

1 lb. ground beef	1 1/2 tsp. Worcestershire sauce
1/3 c. chili sauce	1 tsp. salt
1 1/2 tsp. prepared mustard	Dash of pepper
1 1/2 tsp. prepared horseradish	4 buns, split
1 tbsp. minced onion	Melted butter

Combine the beef, chili sauce, mustard, horseradish, onion, Worcestershire sauce and seasonings and mix well. Spread on the buns, then brush with butter. Place on a broiler rack. Broil 2 inches from heat for about 6 minutes or until brown. 8 servings.

Mrs. Camilla Hayes, Olive Hill, Kentucky

BURGER BROIL

Margarine	1 tsp. salt
4 English muffin halves	1/4 tsp. pepper
3 tsp. prepared mustard	1 tbsp. minced onion
1/2 lb. ground chuck	3 slices Cheddar cheese, cut in
1/4 c. milk	strips

Spread the margarine on the muffin halves, then spread with the mustard. Mix the chuck, milk, salt, pepper and onion together and spread on muffin halves to edges. Top each muffin with cheese. Broil for 7 minutes or until cheese is melted, brushing occasionally with melted margarine. Banana chunks and pineapple chunks, brushed with margarine, may be broiled with beef mixture. 2-4 servings.

Velma Brase, Tulsa, Oklahoma

DELUXE BEEF SANDWICHES

1 lb. ground beef	3/4 tsp. dry mustard
1 c. grated Cheddar cheese	1 sm. onion, minced
3 tbsp. catsup	4 hamburger rolls, split
1/4 tsp. salt	

Combine all the ingredients except the rolls and mix well. Spread to edges of rolls, then place on cookie sheet. Broil 5 to 6 inches from heat for 8 to 10 minutes. May be spread on party rye bread for appetizers. 8 sandwiches.

Mrs. Verna Carter, Lake Charles, Louisiana

FIVE-MINUTE BEEF SANDWICH

1 lb. ground beef	6 slices bread
2 tbsp. grated onion	Butter
1 tsp. salt	Prepared mustard
1/8 tsp. pepper	

Combine the beef, onion, salt and pepper and mix well. Toast bread on one side. Spread the butter on untoasted side of bread, then spread with mustard. Cover each slice with ground beef mixture and place on broiler rack. Broil 3 inches from heat for 5 minutes. 6 servings.

Mrs. Kathy Vance, Fairmont, West Virginia

HERO BURGERS

1 1/2 lb. ground beef	1 tbsp. Worcestershire sauce
1 can tomato soup	1 tsp. horseradish
1/3 c. chopped onion	1 tsp. salt
1 tbsp. prepared mustard	Toasted buns

Combine all the ingredients except the buns and mix well. Spread on the buns, covering edges completely. Broil 4 inches from heat for about 12 minutes. Top with sliced tomato and cheese if desired, then broil till cheese melts.

Mrs. Terri Nolan, Annapolis, Maryland

HOT SUBMARINE SANDWICHES

1 lb. ground beef	1/2 tsp. garlic salt
1/2 c. tomato soup	1/8 tsp. oregano
2 tbsp. minced onion	1 loaf French bread
1/4 tsp. dry mustard	American cheese slices
1/4 tsp. pepper	Tomato slices
1 tsp. salt	

Saute the ground beef until lightly browned, then add the soup, onion, mustard, pepper, salt, garlic salt and oregano. Cut the bread in half lengthwise and cover both halves with beef mixture. Place under broiler for about 20 minutes. Arrange the cheese and tomato slices alternately on beef mixture. Broil until the cheese melts.

Mrs. Sally Scott, Flagstaff, Arizona

JACK BURGERS

9 slices bread	1 sm. onion, chopped
1 lb. hamburger	3 tsp. horseradish mustard
1 egg	Salt and pepper to taste

Place slices of the bread on broiler pan, 3 inches from heat. Broil for 5 minutes or until toasted on one side. Combine the hamburger and egg in a mixing bowl, then add the remaining ingredients and mix thoroughly. Spread thinly over untoasted side of bread. Broil until edge of bread is slightly brown and hamburger mixture is done. 4-5 servings.

Mrs. Maybelle Joiner, Warner Robins, Georgia

SPREAD-A-BURGERS

1 1/2 lb. ground beef	1 tbsp. Worcestershire sauce
1 can mushroom or tomato soup	1 tsp. ground horseradish
1/3 c. finely chopped onion	1 tsp. salt
1 tbsp. prepared mustard	Hot dog buns, halved

Combine all the ingredients except the buns and mix well. Spread to the edges of the buns, then place on broiler rack. Broil until bubbly. 4-5 servings.

Mrs. Leo W. Schroeder, Middle River, Maryland

PIZZABURGERS

1 lb. hamburger	1 lb. grated mozzarella cheese
8 sliced hamburger buns	1/2 green pepper, minced
2 8-oz. cans tomato sauce	1 sm. onion, minced
1 tsp. oregano	Grated Parmesan cheese
1/4 tsp. salt	

Saute the hamburger until lightly browned. Place bun halves on broiler pan. Combine the tomato sauce, oregano and salt and mix. Spread on the bun halves. Sprinkle the mozzarella cheese over the sauce, then cover with hamburger. Sprinkle with the green pepper, onion and Parmesan cheese. Broil until the cheese bubbles. May sprinkle with mushrooms, ripe olives, anchovies, fresh tomatoes or other pizza toppings. 16 servings.

Mrs. Helen Kent, Decatur, Georgia

PIZZA SANDWICH

1 1/4 lb. hamburger	Oregano
1 can spaghetti sauce with mushrooms	1 sm. package grated mozzarella cheese
8 English muffins, split	

Saute the hamburger until browned, then add the spaghetti sauce. Spread on the muffins, then sprinkle with oregano. Cover with cheese, and place on broiler rack. Broil until cheese melts. 16 servings.

Mrs. Edna Thacker, Benton, Arkansas

PIZZABURGER-BY-THE-YARD

1 lb. ground beef	1 5 1/2-oz. can pizza sauce
1/3 c. finely chopped onion	1 loaf French bread, halved
1 clove of garlic, minced	lengthwise
Salt	2 or 3 tomatoes, thinly sliced
Dash of pepper	5 slices sharp process American
1 tsp. oregano	cheese, halved
1/2 tsp. aniseed (opt.)	

Combine the beef, onion, garlic, 1 teaspoon salt, pepper, oregano, aniseed and pizza sauce and mix well. Spread on bread, covering edges well and building up sides slightly. Place on baking sheet. Broil about 6 inches from source of heat for 10 minutes or till beef is done. Sprinkle tomato slices with salt. Overlap tomatoes and cheese slices on beef mixture. Broil just until cheese begins to melt. 8-10 servings.

Mrs. Doris White, New Orleans, Louisiana

VIP CHEESEBURGERS AND FRIES

2 lb. ground beef	Toast points
2 2 1/4-oz. cans deviled ham	2 tbsp. minced parsley
1/2 tsp. hot sauce	Cheddar cheese spread in
1/4 tsp. coarsely ground pepper	pressure can
3/4 c. dry red wine	Frozen French-fried potatoes
1/4 c. butter	Sauteed whole mushrooms

Combine the beef, ham, hot sauce and pepper and mix well. Shape into 4 patties. Place in a flat dish and pour the wine over the patties. Marinate in the refrigerator for 2 hours. Drain, reserving the wine. Melt the butter in a skillet and brown the patties on both sides, then add the reserved wine. Cook to desired degree of doneness and place on toast points. Sprinkle with the parsley, then spoon pan juices over top. Top with rosette of cheese. Prepare the French fries according to package directions and serve with patties. Garnish with mushrooms.

Photograph for this recipe on page 42.

VIENNA BURGERS

1 loaf French Vienna bread	3/4 lb. ground beef
1 egg, beaten	1/4 c. grated onion
1/2 tsp. salt	1/2 c. butter, softened
1 tbsp. Worcestershire sauce	3 tbsp. blue cheese

Slice the bread lengthwise and toast under broiler. Combine the egg, salt, Worcestershire sauce, beef and onion and mix well. Spread on bread. Broil about 4 inches from heat until brown and done. Cream the butter and cheese together, then spread on beef mixture. Place under broiler for 2 minutes, then cut each slice in half and serve with relishes. 4 servings.

Mrs. Mary Lou Butler, Ocala, Florida

GRILL BURGERS

1/4 c. water	10 hamburger buns
1 env. dry onion soup mix	10 tomato slices
2 lb. ground beef	10 dill pickle slices

Combine the water and soup mix, then add the ground beef and mix well. Shape into 10 patties and place on grill. Cook until done. Place patties on buns and add 1 slice tomato and 1 slice pickle to each bun. 10 servings.

Mrs. Paula Cabot, Orlando, Florida

HEARTY RIPE OLIVEBURGERS

1 c. grated Cheddar cheese	1/4 tsp. pepper
2 tbsp. light cream	2 tsp. prepared mustard
3/4 c. canned pitted California ripe olives	1 1/2 lb. lean ground beef
	1 tbsp. oil
1/4 c. chopped green onion	4 hamburger rolls
1 1/2 tsp. salt	Butter

Mix the cheese with the cream. Cut 1/2 cup of the ripe olives into wedges and add to the cheese mixture, then set aside. Chop the remaining olives and mix with the onion, salt, pepper, mustard and ground beef. Shape into 8 thin patties, about 1/2 inch larger in diameter than rolls. Brown the patties on both sides in hot oil. Split rolls and spread with butter, then toast lightly. Top the patties with the cheese mixture and place on broiler pan. Broil until cheese is melted. Place 1 patty on bottom half of roll. Top with another patty and cover with roll top. Garnish with a whole ripe olive. 4 servings.

Hearty Ripe Oliveburgers (above)

Grill Burgers (below)

GRILL BURGERS

1/4 c. water	10 seeded hamburger buns,
1 envelope dry onion soup mix	toasted
2 lb. ground beef	10 slices fresh tomato
Fresh lettuce	Fresh onion rings

Combine the water and soup mix, then add the beef and mix well. Shape into 10 patties and place on grill. Cook to desired degree of doneness. Arrange lettuce on the bottom halves of buns. Place the patties on the lettuce, then add 1 tomato slice and onion rings to each bun. Add the bun tops and serve immediately.

HAMBURGER MAXIMUS

2 slices bread	Lettuce leaves
2 lb. ground beef chuck	4 cheese slices
1/4 c. minced onion	4 hamburger buns
1 egg	4 tomato slices
2 tsp. salt	Onion slices
1 tbsp. Worcestershire sauce	

Soak the bread in water, then squeeze dry and add the beef, onion, egg, salt and Worcestershire sauce. Mix well and shape into 8 patties. Grill on both sides over hot coals to desired degree of doneness. Arrange lettuce on bun half, then add 1 cheese slice. Cover with hamburger patty, 1 tomato slice, 1 onion slice and another hamburger patty. Garnish top with onion rings and mustard. Repeat with remaining ingredients.

Photograph for this recipe on page 2.

BURGERS IN BOLOGNA BOATS

1 lb. ground beef	4 hamburger buns, split and
4 lge. thin slices bologna	toasted
4 slices sharp process American	Mustard
cheese, cut into strips	

Shape the beef into 4 patties the size of the bologna slices. Place over low coals on grill and cook to desired degree of doneness, turning once. Sprinkle with salt and pepper. Slip each patty onto a slice of bologna. Grill till bologna is lightly browned and edges cup around patty. Form lattice on patties with cheese strips. Spread bottom halves of buns with mustard, then add the patties and cover with bun tops. 4 servings.

Jimmie Rae Hankins, Lexington, Alabama

FRENCH MEAT ROLL

1 sm. can evaporated milk	1 1/2 tsp. salt
1 1/2 lb. ground beef	3/4 tbsp. monosodium glutamate
1/2 c. bread crumbs	1 loaf French bread
1 egg	1 c. grated cheese
1 tbsp. mustard	

Combine all the ingredients except the bread and cheese and mix well. Split the French bread in half lengthwise and place on foil. Shape the beef mixture into thin loaves and place on top of the bread. Cover with cheese. Bake at 350 degrees for 25 minutes. 8 servings.

Mrs. Homer Ayers, Roanoke, Virginia

HERO HAMBURGERS

2 lb. ground beef	1/2 c. grated American cheese
2 eggs, lightly beaten	1/4 c. pickle relish
1/2 tsp. salt	1 1/2 c. chopped onion
1 c. barbecue sauce	8 hamburger buns

Combine the beef, eggs, salt and 1/2 cup barbecue sauce and mix lightly. Divide into 16 portions, then gently shape into thick round patties. Place about 1 teaspoon each cheese, relish, onion and remaining barbecue sauce on half of the patties, then top with remaining patties. Press edges together to seal in filling. Broil for about 5 minutes on each side, basting with remaining sauce after turning. Serve in buns. 8 servings.

Sharon Thomas, Proctor, Arkansas

Onionburgers (below)

ONIONBURGERS

1 1/2 c. chopped onions	1 1/2 tsp. salt
2 tbsp. butter or margarine	1 1/2 lb. ground beef
2 tbsp. prepared horseradish	1/4 tsp. pepper
2 tbsp. prepared mustard	

Saute the onions lightly in the butter. Combine the onion mixture, horseradish, mustard and 1/2 teaspoon salt and mix well. Combine the ground beef with the pepper and remaining salt and mix well. Shape into 12 patties. Spread the onion mixture on 6 patties, then top with remaining patties and seal edges together. Chill thoroughly. Place on broiler rack in broiler pan. Broil, 2 inches from source of heat, for 8 to 10 minutes or until brown. Turn and brown on second side. Serve with cucumbers and tomato slices.

HOT MEAT LOAF SANDWICHES

1 lb. ground beef	1 can vegetable soup
1/4 tsp. monosodium glutamate	4 frankfurter buns, split
1 slice bread, crumbled	Butter or margarine

Preheat oven to 450 degrees. Combine the beef, monosodium glutamate and bread in bowl, then stir in the soup and mix well. Shape mixture into four 1/2-inch thick oval patties and place on a baking sheet. Bake for 10 minutes. Spread the cut surfaces of buns with butter and place on the baking sheet with patties. Bake for 5 minutes longer. Arrange buns on heated platter, then place patties on buns. 4 servings.

Mrs. Lorene Loftin, Gadsden, Alabama

PEANUTBURGERS

2 lb. lean ground beef	2 c. finely chopped roasted
1 tsp. salt	peanuts
1 tbsp. steak sauce	2 tbsp. chopped onion
4 slices bacon, cut in half	2 tbsp. chopped parsley

Season the ground beef with salt and steak sauce and shape into 16 patties. Saute the bacon in a skillet until light brown. Combine the peanuts, onion and parsley and mix well. Place on 8 patties and top with 1 piece of bacon. Cover with remaining patties and press edges together. Place in a shallow baking pan. Broil for about 5 minutes. Turn and broil for 5 minutes longer or until browned. 8 servings.

Mrs. Bruce Wallace, Ashville, North Carolina

RHINE BURGER STACKS

1 lb. ground beef	1/2 c. well-drained sauerkraut
1 tsp. salt	8 slices bacon
1/4 tsp. caraway seed	8 slices pumpernickel bread,
1/8 tsp. pepper	buttered

Mix the ground beef lightly with salt, caraway seed and pepper, then shape into 8 patties, about 1/2 inch thick. Place 2 tablespoons sauerkraut on 4 patties and top with the remaining patties. Wrap 2 slices bacon around each patty and fasten with moistened wooden picks. Broil, 4 inches from heat, for 6 minutes on each side for medium or until bacon is crisp and beef is of desired degree of doneness. Place between 2 slices of bread. 4 servings.

Mrs. Martha McCoy, Fort Worth, Texas

PIZZA LOAF

1 1-lb. long loaf French bread	1 tsp. salt
Butter or margarine, softened	1/8 tsp. pepper
3/4 lb. ground beef	1 1/2 tbsp. minced onion
1/2 c. grated Parmesan cheese	1 15-oz. can tomato sauce
1/2 tsp. oregano	8 slices process cheese

Cut the bread in half lengthwise and spread with butter. Combine the beef, Parmesan cheese, seasonings, onion and tomato sauce and mix well. Spread on cut sides of bread, then place on cookie sheet. Bake at 350 degrees for 20 minutes. Top with cheese. Bake for about 5 minutes or until cheese is melted. 8-10 servings.

Mrs. Lori Nelson, Shawnee, Oklahoma

Teepee Burgers (below)

TEEPEE BURGERS

2 lb. ground beef	Butter
2 tsp. monosodium glutamate	Lettuce
1 1/2 tsp. salt	Prepared mustard
1/2 tsp. pepper	8 slices onion
8 slices process American cheese	8 slices tomato
16 slices rye bread or 8 hamburger buns	Pickle relish
	8 stuffed olives

Break up the beef with fork in mixing bowl and sprinkle with monosodium glutamate, salt and pepper. Toss gently with fork to distribute seasonings. Shape into 8 patties. Panbroil, broil or grill to desired degree of doneness. Top with cheese just before hamburgers are done. Spread the bread with butter and cover with lettuce. Top with hamburger patty, then spread with mustard and top with onion and tomato. Spread with pickle relish, then top with olive. Cover with bread slice. Repeat for each serving. 8 servings.

BARBECUED SLAWBURGERS

2 lb. ground beef	5 to 6 tbsp. brown sugar
1 med. onion, diced	Buns
1 bottle barbecue sauce	Coleslaw
1 sauce bottle water	

Brown the ground beef and onion in small amount of hot fat, then add the barbecue sauce, water and brown sugar. Bring to a boil and simmer for 2 hours. Serve on buns with coleslaw. 10-12 servings.

Mrs. Laura Higdon, Covington, Kentucky

GINNEY'S BARBECUE BURGERS

1 lge. onion, chopped	3 tbsp. Worcestershire sauce
1 1/2 lb. ground beef, crumbled	2 tbsp. prepared mustard
3 tbsp. bacon drippings	2 tsp. salt
1 c. tomato juice	1/4 tsp. pepper
1/2 c. water	1/2 c. hickory barbecue sauce
1/4 c. vinegar	Hamburger buns
1/4 c. (firmly packed) brown sugar	

Cook the onion and ground beef in bacon drippings in deep frypan or Dutch oven over medium heat until onion is tender. Add the next 8 ingredients and simmer for 15 minutes. Add the barbecue sauce and cook for 5 minutes longer. Serve over toasted hamburger buns.

Virginia Green, Tulsa, Oklahoma

HAMBURGER STROGANOFF BUNS

1 lb. ground beef	1/4 tsp. pepper
1 tsp. onion powder	1/4 tsp. paprika
1/4 c. butter	1 can sliced mushrooms
2 tbsp. flour	1 can cream of chicken soup
2 tsp. salt	1 c. sour cream
1/4 tsp. monosodium glutamate	6 hard rolls

Break the beef into small pieces in a skillet, then add the onion powder, butter, flour, salt, monosodium glutamate, pepper and paprika and saute for 5 to 10 minutes, stirring frequently. Add the mushrooms and soup, then simmer for 10 minutes. Stir in the sour cream and heat through. Cut slice from top of rolls and hollow out inside. Fill the rolls with ground beef mixture. Garnish with snipped parsley or chives. 6 servings.

Mrs. Elsie Hawkins, Baton Rouge, Louisiana

OLIVEBURGERS

1 onion, chopped	1 sm. can chopped black olives
2 lb. hamburger	1 sm. can chopped stuffed olives
1 lge. can spaghetti sauce with	1 lb. mild cheese, grated
mushrooms	Salt and pepper to taste
4 hard-cooked eggs, chopped	Hamburger buns

Brown the onion and hamburger in a large frypan, then pour off excess fat. Add the spaghetti sauce and simmer for 20 to 25 minutes. Cool. Add the eggs, olives, cheese, salt and pepper, then fill the buns. Wrap each bun in foil. Bake at 350 degrees for about 15 minutes or until cheese melts. Buns may be frozen but reheat for about 40 minutes.

Mrs. Dolly Simpson, Columbus, Georgia

Texas Joe (below)

TEXAS JOE

1 lb. cooked roast beef	2 tbsp. chili powder
2 1/2 lb. ground beef	1 1/2 tsp. salt
1 med. onion, chopped	1/4 tsp. pepper
1 clove of garlic, minced	1/4 tsp. crushed hot red
3 8-oz. cans tomato sauce	pepper
2 tbsp. prepared mustard	1 16-oz. can red or kidney
2 tbsp. vinegar	beans

Slice the roast into thin slivers. Brown the ground beef, onion and garlic lightly in frying pan, then pour off the drippings. Combine the tomato sauce, mustard, vinegar, chili powder, salt, pepper and red pepper and mix well. Add the tomato sauce mixture and beans to ground beef, then cover and simmer for 25 minutes. Add the roast beef to ground beef mixture and cook for 5 minutes longer or until heated through. Serve on hard rolls. 8 cups.

PIZZA SUB

1 lb. ground beef	Dash of pepper
1 tbsp. salad oil	1 No. 2 can tomatoes
1 onion, chopped	1 6-oz. can tomato paste
1 tbsp. parsley flakes	18 hard rolls, split
1 tbsp. basil	1 lb. mozzarella cheese, sliced
2 tsp. salt	

Brown the beef in oil in a skillet, then add the remaining ingredients except rolls and cheese. Simmer, covered, for 1 hour. Spread on both halves of the rolls, then top bottom half with cheese and press halves together. Bake for 10 minutes in 350-degree oven. Cut long rolls in half before serving.

Mrs. Charles Chalmers, Jr., Baltimore, Maryland

SANDWICH STROGANOFF

1 tsp. salt	1/4 c. chili sauce
1 lb. ground beef	3/4 c. sour cream
1/4 c. chopped onion	1/2 loaf French bread, sliced
1/4 tsp. garlic juice	lengthwise
1/4 tsp. pepper	Tomato slices or green pepper
1/2 tsp. Worcestershire sauce	rings
2 tbsp. flour	Grated cheese

Preheat the skillet, then sprinkle in the salt and add the ground beef and onion. Cook, stirring, until brown, then add the garlic juice, pepper and Worcestershire sauce. Stir in the flour and chili sauce and cook, stirring, until well blended. Reduce heat and blend in the sour cream. Spoon onto the bread, then garnish with tomato slices and cheese. Broil until cheese is melted. Slice into 6 servings. Serve immediately.

Mrs. Martha Clinton, Blytheville, Arkansas

SATURDAY NIGHT SPECIAL

1 lb. ground beef	2 tbsp. prepared mustard
1/2 c. chopped onions	2 tbsp. catsup
1 tbsp. fat	Salt and pepper to taste
1 can chicken gumbo soup	

Brown the ground beef and onions in hot fat, then add the remaining ingredients. Cook until onions are done and mixture is thickened. Serve between hamburger buns.

Mrs. Forrest H. Brown, Huntsville, Alabama

SUPER BURGERS

1 lb. ground beef	1/3 c. catsup
1 chopped onion	Hamburger buns, split
1/8 tsp. oregano	Cheese slices
1 can minestrone soup	

Brown the beef and onion in a skillet. Add the oregano, soup and catsup and simmer for 5 to 10 minutes. Place on bun halves and place a cheese slice on each half. Broil for about 2 minutes.

Mrs. Gloria M. Kite, Stanley, Virginia

Carrot Meat Loaf (page 60)

loaves

Meat loaf is one of the most dependable and best-loved of all ground beef dishes. There are as many kinds of meat loaf as there are family preferences. Now the best of these recipes from southern families are yours to share in this section.

Feature Barbecued Meat Loaf — a hotly seasoned dish that is prepared the way Southerners like it! Or combine two favorite southern foods to make Individual Meat Loaves with Peaches, a flavor blend that will have your family asking for "more, please!" And on those warm evenings when you don't want to turn on the oven, serve Top-of-the-Stove Meat Loaf — it's an easily prepared dish that will turn your meal into an adventure.

You'll find unusual meat loaf recipes in these pages, too, like the one for Ravioli Stuffed Meat Loaf. Serve it at your next buffet party and enjoy the compliments which follow. When you want a real taste treat, feature Avocado-Tomato Meat Loaf. Its blend of flavors, colors, and textures is certain to make it the center of attraction whenever it appears.

There are many, many more exciting meat loaf recipes awaiting you in this section. Every one is a home-tested, dependable dish you'll delight in serving to your family and friends!

BEEF LOAF SUPREME

1 2 1/2-oz. can sliced mushrooms	1/2 tsp. monosodium glutamate
Milk	1/8 tsp. pepper
1 egg, lightly beaten	1/4 c. minced onion
1 1/2 c. soft bread crumbs	2 tbsp. finely chopped green pepper
2/3 c. catsup	1 1/2 lb. ground beef chuck
1 1/2 tsp. salt	1/2 tsp. prepared mustard

Drain the mushrooms and reserve the juice, then add enough milk to the reserved juice to make 1/2 cup liquid. Combine the milk mixture with the egg, bread crumbs, 1/3 cup catsup, salt, monosodium glutamate, pepper, onion and green pepper and mix well. Add the beef and beat with a fork until well mixed. Turn into an oiled 8 1/2 x 4 1/2 x 2 1/2-inch loaf pan, packing lightly into pan. Turn out onto oiled shallow pan. Bake at 400 degrees for 40 minutes. Combine the remaining catsup and the mustard. Remove the loaf from oven and arrange the mushrooms over the loaf, then spread the catsup mixture over top. Bake for 10 minutes longer. 6-8 servings.

Photograph for this recipe on cover.

CARROT MEAT LOAF

3 lb. ground beef	1 lge. potato, grated
1 lge. onion, grated	2 eggs
3 carrots, grated	Soy sauce
1 sm. package saltines, finely crushed	Salt and pepper to taste
	2 tbsp. honey

Combine the first 6 ingredients, then add 1/2 cup soy sauce and season with salt and pepper. Mix well, then pack into a large loaf pan. Unmold onto a shallow baking pan. Brush top with soy sauce. Bake at 350 degrees for 1 hour and 15 minutes then brush with the honey. Bake for 15 minutes longer.

Photograph for this recipe on page 58.

BEEF LOAF

2 lb. ground beef	2 tbsp. chopped green pepper
1/2 c. non-dairy coffee creamer	3/4 c. catsup
1 egg white	2 1/4 tsp. salt
1 c. quick-cooking oats	Dash of pepper
2 tbsp. chopped onion	1/2 tsp. monosodium glutamate

Combine all ingredients in a bowl and mix well. Pack into a 9 1/2 x 5 x 3-inch loaf pan. Bake at 350 degrees for 1 hour and 20 minutes. Score top and pour small amount of additional catsup into scores. Bake for 10 minutes longer.

Justine Wendt, Hundred, West Virginia

BARBECUED MEAT LOAF

1 lb. hamburger	Pepper to taste
2 lge. eggs, beaten	1/4 tsp. Worcestershire sauce
1 lge. onion, diced	1/4 tsp. thyme
1 green pepper, diced	1 c. cracker meal
2 stalks celery, diced	1 sm. can tomato sauce with cheese
1/2 sm. can blanched almonds	Barbecue sauce
Garlic salt to taste	

Mix all ingredients except barbecue sauce and pack in loaf pan firmly. Brush with barbecue sauce. Bake at 300 degrees for 1 hour and 30 minutes, brushing occasionally with barbecue sauce.

Mrs. Philip A. Cowen, Hendersonville, North Carolina

FRESH POTATO-FROSTED MEAT LOAF

1 1/2 lb. ground beef	1 egg, slightly beaten
1 can cream of chicken soup	1/2 tsp. salt
1 c. bread crumbs	Dash of pepper
1/4 c. finely chopped fresh onion	2 c. mashed fresh potatoes
	1/4 c. water

Combine the beef, 1/2 cup soup, crumbs, onion, egg, salt and pepper and mix thoroughly. Shape firmly into a loaf and place in a shallow baking pan. Bake at 350 degrees for 1 hour. Frost loaf with the mashed potatoes and bake for 15 minutes longer. Blend the remaining soup and water and heat thoroughly. Serve with the meat loaf.

Fresh Potato-Frosted Meat Loaf (above)

BEEF AND POTATO LOAF

3 c. ground beef	2 tbsp. chopped parsley
3 c. mashed potatoes	2 tbsp. shortening
1 c. milk	Salt and pepper to taste
2 tbsp. chopped onion	3 eggs, separated

Mix the beef, potatoes and milk in a bowl. Saute the onion and parsley in shortening in a saucepan until tender, then add to the beef mixture. Mix in the salt, pepper and beaten egg yolks. Fold in beaten egg whites. Pack into a greased baking dish. Bake at 350 degrees for 1 hour. 6 servings.

Sheila Arrington, Gilmer, Texas

BLENDER MEAT LOAF

1 lge. onion	1 egg
1 lge. potato	1 1/2 lb. ground beef
1 green pepper	2 tsp. salt
1/2 c. diced celery	1/2 tsp. pepper
1/4 c. milk	1/2 tsp. monosodium glutamate

Dice the onion, potato and green pepper and place in a blender container. Add the celery, milk and egg. Blend at low speed until vegetables are a coarse pulp, then place in a bowl. Add remaining ingredients and mix well. Shape into a loaf and place in well-greased baking pan. Bake in 350-degree oven for 1 hour. 6 servings.

Mrs. Ruth Yelvington, Corsicana, Texas

STEAK TARTARE

1 lb. ground top round beef	1 egg
1 tsp. monosodium glutamate	1 tsp. salt
1 tbsp. finely chopped onion	1/8 tsp. pepper

Combine all of the ingredients and blend well. Shape into an oval in the center of serving platter and score the top. Garnish with tomato wedges, chopped onion, capers and watercress. Serve with rye bread slices or crisp crackers. 24 servings.

Photograph for this recipe on page 9.

CHEESEBURGER LOAF

1/2 c. evaporated milk	1 1/2 tsp. salt
1 egg	1 tsp. dry mustard
1 c. cracker crumbs	1 tbsp. catsup
1 1/2 lb. ground beef	1 c. grated American cheese
2 tbsp. chopped onion	

Combine all ingredients except the cheese in a bowl and mix thoroughly. Line a loaf pan with heavy waxed paper. Place 1/2 cup cheese in bottom of pan and cover with half the beef mixture. Repeat layers. Bake at 350 degrees for about 1 hour. Let stand for 10 minutes before turning out on a platter. Remove waxed paper and slice. 6 servings.

Mrs. Dale M. Dickey, Sadler, Texas

OLIVE-STUFFED BEEF LOAF

1 1/4 lb. ground beef	1/4 c. water
Salt and pepper to taste	12 pimento-stuffed olives
2 cooked potatoes, mashed	1 1/4 c. tomato juice
2 eggs, beaten	1/4 c. sherry or Madeira
1/4 c. light cream	2 tsp. flour

Mix the ground beef, salt, pepper, potatoes and eggs in a bowl. Add the cream and water and mix well. Place in a greased loaf pan and press the olives into beef mixture. Cover with foil. Bake at 350 degrees for 1 hour. Remove from pan and place on a platter. Chill. Mix the tomato juice and sherry in a saucepan and bring to a boil. Mix the flour with 1 tablespoon water until smooth, then stir into the tomato mixture. Add salt and pepper and cook until thickened. Chill. Pour the sauce over the meat loaf and garnish with sliced olives. May be served hot, if desired. 4 servings.

Olive-Stuffed Beef Loaf (above)

Meat Loaf with Zesty Topping (below)

MEAT LOAF WITH ZESTY TOPPING

3/4 c. milk
1 1/2 c. soft bread crumbs
2 lb. ground beef
2 tsp. salt
1/8 tsp. pepper
1 med. carrot, grated

1 sm. onion, diced
2 eggs, beaten
1/4 c. catsup
3 tbsp. brown sugar
2 tbsp. prepared mustard

Pour the milk over the bread crumbs, then add the ground beef, salt, pepper, carrot, onion and eggs and mix thoroughly. Pack in a 9 x 5-inch loaf pan. Mix the catsup, brown sugar and mustard together and spread on meat loaf. Bake at 300 degrees for 1 hour and 30 minutes to 1 hour and 45 minutes. Top with cooked green pepper rings, if desired. 8 servings.

CHILI-BEEF LOAF

2 lb. ground beef
1 pkg. chili seasoning mix
1 egg, slightly beaten
1 med. onion, chopped

1 8-oz. can tomato sauce with
   cheese
1/2 tsp. salt
Catsup

Combine all ingredients except catsup in a bowl and mix well. Shape into a loaf and place in a baking pan. Spread layer of catsup over top. Bake at 375 degrees for 1 hour.

Mrs. William K. Livesay, Church Hill, Tennessee

APRICOT MEAT LOAF

2 lb. ground beef
1 c. chopped dried apricots
1/2 c. dry bread crumbs
2 eggs
2 tbsp. chopped parsley

1 1/2 tsp. salt
1/8 tsp. pepper
1/2 c. brown sugar
1 tsp. water

Combine all ingredients except the brown sugar and water and shape into a loaf. Place in a greased shallow pan. Bake at 350 degrees for 1 hour. Mix the brown sugar with water in a saucepan and heat until sugar is melted. Spread over meat loaf and bake for 5 to 10 minutes longer. 8 servings.

Diana Shelby, Charleston, West Virginia

AVOCADO-TOMATO MEAT LOAF

4 slices bacon
3/4 c. diced celery
1/2 c. chopped green onions
2 tbsp. minced parsley
1/2 c. diced green pepper
1 lb. ground veal
1 lb. hamburger
1 8-oz. can tomato sauce

1 c. bread crumbs
2 c. chopped mushrooms
1 egg, slightly beaten
2 tbsp. flour
1 peeled avocado, diced
2 tsp. celery salt
1/2 tsp. pepper

Fry the bacon in a skillet until brown, then remove from skillet. Add the celery, green onions, parsley and green pepper to bacon drippings and cook until tender. Place in a bowl. Mix in remaining ingredients and pack into a 5 x 5 x 9-inch loaf pan. Bake at 350 degrees for 45 minutes. Drain and bake for 45 minutes longer. 6 servings.

Laura Crosby, Biloxi, Mississippi

MEAT LOAF WITH PINEAPPLE

2 lb. ground beef
1/2 c. chopped onion
1/4 c. chopped celery
1 c. soft bread crumbs
1 egg, beaten

1 tsp. salt
Pepper to taste
Catsup
1/2 c. pineapple juice
2 or 3 slices pineapple

Combine the beef, onion, celery, bread crumbs, egg, salt and pepper in a bowl. Add 1/2 cup catsup and pineapple juice and mix well. Pack into a loaf pan and cover with a layer of catsup. Garnish with pineapple slices. Bake at 350 degrees for about 1 hour and 30 minutes.

Mrs. B. C. Flarity, Cloudland, Georgia

CRANBERRY MEAT LOAF

1 lb. ground beef	1 1/2 tsp. salt
1 c. cooked rice	2 c. whole cranberry sauce
1/2 c. tomato juice	1/3 c. sugar
1 egg, slightly beaten	1 tbsp. lemon juice
1/4 c. chopped onion	

Combine the ground beef, rice, tomato juice, egg, onion and salt. Shape into a loaf and place in a baking pan. Mix remaining ingredients and pour over loaf. Bake at 350 degrees for 45 minutes to 1 hour. 6-8 servings.

Mrs. Wanda Brian, Weatherford, Texas

INDIVIDUAL MEAT LOAVES WITH PEACHES

3/4 c. rolled oats	5 tbsp. Worcestershire sauce
1 1/2 lb. ground beef	1 No. 2 1/2 can peach halves,
1 2/3 c. evaporated milk	drained
1 1/2 tsp. salt	Whole cloves
1/4 tsp. pepper	Brown sugar
1/4 c. finely chopped onions	Vinegar
1/4 c. chili sauce or catsup	1 can cream of mushroom soup

Mix the oats, ground beef, 1 cup milk, salt, pepper, onions, chili sauce and 4 tablespoons Worcestershire sauce and shape into 6 loaves. Place in a well-greased shallow pan. Bake at 350 degrees for about 45 minutes. Stud the peach halves with cloves. Sprinkle lightly with brown sugar and pour 1/2 teaspoon vinegar into cavity of each half. Place peaches around meat loaves and bake for 15 minutes longer. Combine remaining milk, soup and remaining Worcestershire sauce in a saucepan and heat through. Serve with meat loaves.

Mrs. M. B. Nichols, Como, Texas

UPSIDE-DOWN MEAT LOAF

Dried apricots	1 tsp. salt
Dried prunes	1/4 tsp. thyme
1 lb. ground round steak	2 onions, finely chopped
1/4 lb. ground veal	1 can vegetable soup
1/2 lb. ground pork	1/4 c. maple syrup
1/4 lb. ground ham	3/4 c. bread crumbs
1 egg, beaten	

Arrange the apricots and prunes in a checkerboard pattern in a greased loaf pan. Mix remaining ingredients and pack in the loaf pan on top of fruits. Bake at 350 degrees for 1 hour and 30 minutes. 8-10 servings.

Mrs. Myra Ross, Baton Rouge, Louisiana

INDIVIDUAL LOAVES WITH PEPPY SAUCE

1 lb. ground beef	1/2 can tomato paste
1/4 c. rolled oats or bread crumbs	1/2 c. water
1/2 c. chopped onion	1/3 c. vinegar
2 1/4 tsp. salt	3 tbsp. molasses
1 tsp. pepper	1 tsp. dry mustard
1 egg	1/4 tsp. cayenne pepper
1/4 c. milk	2 tbsp. Worcestershire sauce

Mix the ground beef, oats, 1/4 cup onion, 1 1/2 teaspoons salt, pepper, egg and milk in a bowl. Shape into 5 loaves. Brown on all sides in a skillet, then place in a baking pan. Combine the tomato paste, water, vinegar, remaining onion, molasses, mustard, remaining salt, cayenne pepper and Worcestershire sauce and pour over loaves. Bake at 350 degrees for 1 hour.

Mrs. B. B. Breeland, Hattiesburg, Mississippi

JUICY MEAT LOAF

1 1/2 lb. ground beef	1 1/2 c. milk
1/2 tsp. salt	1/2 stick margarine
1 sm. onion, finely chopped	1 tbsp. (heaping) flour
1 lge. egg	1 sm. can tomato sauce
1/2 c. chopped celery	1/2 c. catsup
1/2 c. rolled oats	1 sm. can mushrooms, drained

Combine the ground beef, salt, onion, egg, celery, oats and 1/2 cup milk in a bowl. Shape into a loaf and place in a baking dish. Melt the margarine in a saucepan and blend in flour. Add remaining milk and cook until thickened, stirring constantly. Remove from heat and add tomato sauce, catsup and mushrooms. Pour over meat loaf. Bake at 425 degrees for 10 minutes. Reduce temperature to 325 degrees and bake for 1 hour and 30 minutes longer. 6 servings.

Mrs. Nelson Conley, Trezevant, Tennessee

BEEF AND OATS LOAF

2 lb. ground beef	2 tsp. salt
1 1/2 c. quick-cooking oats	1/2 med. mango pepper, chopped
2 eggs, beaten	1 med. onion, chopped
1 sm. can tomato puree	1 pkg. brown gravy mix

Mix the ground beef, oats, eggs, tomato puree, salt, mango pepper and onion in a large bowl. Shape into a loaf and place in a baking dish. Bake at 400 degrees for 25 minutes. Prepare the gravy mix according to package directions and pour half the gravy over meat loaf. Bake for 25 minutes longer. Slice the meat loaf and serve with remaining gravy.

Mrs. Cleva Harper, Falmouth, Kentucky

LITTLE SHERRIED LOAVES

1 1/2 lb. hamburger	1 tbsp. cornstarch
1 egg, slightly beaten	2 tbsp. brown sugar
1 c. bread crumbs	1 beef bouillon cube
3 tbsp. chopped onion	3/4 c. hot water
1 8-oz. can tomato sauce	3/4 c. sherry
1 1/2 tsp. salt	1 tbsp. vinegar
1/4 tsp. pepper	1 tsp. prepared mustard

Mix the hamburger, egg, bread crumbs, onion, 1/2 can tomato sauce, salt and pepper and shape into 4 loaves. Place in a shallow baking dish. Bake at 350 degrees for 40 minutes, then drain. Combine the cornstarch with brown sugar in a saucepan. Dissolve the bouillon cube in the hot water, then stir into the cornstarch mixture. Add the sherry, vinegar and mustard and cook, stirring, until thick. Pour over loaves and bake for 30 minutes longer, basting every 5 minutes.

Mrs. E. P. Brewton, Anniston, Alabama

MEAT LOAF DINNER

2 slices bread	1 sm. onion, chopped
1 lb. ground beef	1 stalk celery, chopped
1 1/2 tsp. salt	2 tbsp. shortening
1/8 tsp. pepper	5 med. potatoes, sliced
1 egg, slightly beaten	4 carrots, sliced

Soak the bread in just enough water to moisten. Add the beef, salt, pepper, egg, onion and celery and mix well. Shape into 2 loaves and wrap in waxed paper. Refrigerate until chilled. Unwrap loaves. Brown in hot shortening in a pressure cooker until brown. Place potatoes and carrots around loaves and add 1 cup water. Cook at 10 pounds pressure for 15 minutes. 6 servings.

Mrs. Jack Ferguson, Murphy, North Carolina

MEAT LOAF WITH PIQUANT SAUCE

2/3 c. dry bread crumbs	1/8 tsp. pepper
1 c. milk	1/2 tsp. sage
1 1/2 lb. ground beef	3 tbsp. brown sugar
2 eggs, beaten	1 tsp. nutmeg
1/4 c. grated onion	1 tsp. mustard
1/2 c. finely chopped green pepper	1/4 c. barbecue sauce
1 tsp. salt	

Soak the bread in milk. Add the beef, eggs, onion, green pepper, salt, pepper and sage and mix well. Shape into a loaf and place in a baking pan. Combine remaining ingredients and spread over meat loaf. Bake at 350 degrees for 1 hour.

Mrs. Ethel Davenport, Norman, Oklahoma

MEAT LOAF WITH SPICY SAUCE

1 1/2 lb. ground beef	1 tbsp. Worcestershire sauce
1 c. corn flakes	1/4 tsp. salt
2 egg yolks	1/2 c. water
2 tsp. instant minced onion	1 tbsp. mustard
1/4 tsp. celery seed	2 tbsp. vinegar
1 c. tomato paste	2 tbsp. brown sugar
1/2 c. milk	Dash of pepper

Combine the beef, corn flakes, egg yolks, onion, celery seed, 1/2 cup tomato paste, milk, Worcestershire sauce and salt in a bowl and mix well. Shape into a loaf and place in a baking pan. Combine the water, remaining tomato paste, mustard, vinegar, brown sugar and pepper and pour over loaf. Bake at 350 degrees for 1 hour and 30 minutes.

Mrs. John Carroll, La Follette, Tennessee

MEAT LOAF WITH VEGETABLES

2 lb. ground beef	3 sm. onions
1/4 c. finely chopped onion	3 carrots, sliced
1/2 c. bread crumbs	4 or 5 potatoes, sliced
2 eggs, well beaten	1/2 c. chopped celery
Salt and pepper to taste	1 can tomato soup
1 can tomato sauce	

Combine the beef, chopped onion, bread crumbs, eggs, salt, pepper and tomato sauce in a bowl, then shape into loaves. Brown in a skillet in small amount of fat. Slice the small onions and separate into rings. Place over meat loaves. Add the carrots, potatoes, celery and tomato soup and simmer for 1 hour.

Mrs. Bertha Pippin, Malvern, Alabama

POT ROAST MEAT LOAF

1 lb. lean ground beef	Pepper
2/3 c. evaporated milk	3 potatoes
1/3 c. fine dry bread crumbs	3 onions
1/4 c. catsup or chili sauce	3 carrots
2 tsp. salt	2 tsp. dried parsley flakes
2 tsp. Worcestershire sauce	

Mix the ground beef, milk, bread crumbs, catsup, 1 teaspoon salt, Worcestershire sauce and 1/4 teaspoon pepper in a mixing bowl. Shape into a loaf and place in center of a 13 x 9 x 2-inch pan. Peel potatoes and onions and slice 1/4 inch thick. Scrape the carrots and cut in quarters. Mix parsley flakes, 1 teaspoon salt and dash of pepper. Place vegetables around meat loaf and sprinkle with salt mixture. Cover tightly with foil. Bake at 375 degrees for 1 hour or until vegetables are tender. Uncover and bake for 10 minutes longer. 6 servings.

Mrs. Raymond Maddox, Moreland, Kentucky

Ripe Olive Birthday Loaf (below)

RIPE OLIVE BIRTHDAY LOAF

1 1/2 lb. lean ground beef	1 2/3 c. canned pitted
1 1/2 c. soft bread crumbs	California ripe olives
2 tbsp. instant minced onion	1/4 c. chopped parsley
1/2 tsp. marjoram, crumbled	Instant mashed potatoes for
1 1/2 tsp. salt	6 servings
1/4 tsp. pepper	1 tbsp. butter
1 egg, lightly beaten	1/2 tsp. onion salt
Milk	2 egg yolks

Preheat oven to 350 degrees. Mix the beef, bread crumbs, onion, marjoram, salt and pepper together. Combine the egg and 2/3 cup milk and mix with the beef mixture thoroughly. Shape into a 9 x 12-inch rectangle on sheet of waxed paper. Drain the olives thoroughly and arrange 4 rows of olives, end to end, across the 12-inch width of beef mixture, starting about 1 inch from edge. Sprinkle with parsley. Roll up, shaping into 9-inch loaf. Place on shallow baking pan. Bake for 45 minutes. Prepare instant potatoes according to package directions, then add the butter and onion salt. Beat the egg yolks until foamy, then add 1/4 cup milk and stir into the potatoes. Remove meat loaf from oven and frost with mashed potatoes. Return to oven and bake for 10 minutes longer. Brown top lightly under broiler, if desired. Garnish with ripe olives. 6-8 servings.

BEEF AND FRENCH FRY LOAF

1 1/2 lb. ground beef	2 tsp. salt
1/2 c. quick-cooking oats	1/8 tsp. pepper
2 eggs, slightly beaten	1 9-oz. package frozen French
1/3 c. chopped onion	fries
1/2 c. chili sauce	1 can cheese soup

Combine all ingredients except the potatoes and cheese soup and divide into 3 portions. Pack 1 portion into bottom of a greased 9 x 5 x 3-inch loaf pan. Press half the potatoes into beef mixture and cover with second portion of beef mixture. Add remaining potatoes, then cover with remaining beef mixture. Bake at 350 degrees for about 1 hour or until done. Let stand for 5 to 10 minutes before removing from pan. Heat the cheese soup and serve with loaf. 6-8 servings.

Mrs. Frances Moorman, Sterlington, Louisiana

CELERY MEAT LOAF

1 celery heart, 2 1/2 in. in diameter	1 tsp. garlic powder
	1 tsp. Worcestershire sauce
Salt to taste	1/2 tsp. chili powder
1 c. grated sharp Cheddar cheese	1/2 tsp. pepper
2 tbsp. finely chopped pimento	2 eggs, slightly beaten
3 lb. ground beef	1/8 tsp. liquid smoke
1/2 c. quick-cooking oats	1/2 c. chopped green onions
1/2 c. evaporated milk	1/4 c. chopped green pepper
1 tbsp. seasoned salt	1 lb. sliced bacon

Cut celery heart to 8 inches long. Wash and drain. Keep bottom of celery heart intact. Pull stalks apart gently and sprinkle with salt. Combine the cheese and pimento and spread between celery stalks. Wrap tightly in foil and chill. Combine remaining ingredients except bacon. Turn out onto a large sheet of waxed paper and pat out to an oval about 11 x 12 1/2 inches. Cut off root of celery heart. Place celery in center of beef mixture and fold beef mixture up and over celery. Pat into roll shape, completely enclosing celery. Place the bacon slices in chevron pattern over top of roll, having slices overlap slightly, then tuck bacon ends underneath, securing with wooden picks, if necessary. Tie roll securely with string and wrap in foil. Seal top but do not close ends. Bake at 350 degrees for about 1 hour and 30 minutes. 10-12 servings.

Mrs. Paul B. Johnson, Jackson, Mississippi

SOUTHERN PECAN-STUFFED MEAT LOAF

2 lb. ground beef	2 c. soft bread crumbs
2 tsp. salt	1 c. chopped pecans
1/4 tsp. pepper	2 tbsp. minced green pepper
2 tbsp. minced onion	1/4 tsp. paprika
1 egg, slightly beaten	1 c. milk
1 tbsp. evaporated milk	French dressing

Combine the ground beef, 1 1/2 teaspoons salt, pepper, onion, egg and evaporated milk and mix thoroughly. Place on aluminum foil and press into rectangular shape 1/2 inch thick. Combine the bread crumbs, pecans, remaining salt, green pepper, paprika and milk and spread over beef mixture. Roll as for jelly roll and place, seam side down, in a loaf pan. Bake at 350 degrees for 1 hour or until done. Brush with French dressing and serve.

Helen N. Roberts, Lineville, Alabama

Oriental Beef Ring (below)

ORIENTAL BEEF RING

2 eggs	2 tsp. salt
1/2 c. milk	2 lb. ground beef
2 c. fresh bread crumbs	1 5-oz. can sliced water
1/4 c. minced onion	chestnuts, drained
1 tbsp. prepared mustard	Curried rice

Beat the eggs lightly and blend in the milk and bread crumbs. Add the remaining ingredients except the rice and mix thoroughly. Shape into an 8-inch ring with a 4-inch hole in the center in a shallow baking dish. Bake at 350 degrees for about 45 minutes. Lift carefully to serving dish. Fill center with the curried rice. Garnish rice with chopped green onion tops.

Curried Apples

3 med. Washington apples	1 tbsp. lemon juice
2 tbsp. butter or margarine	1 tbsp. cornstarch
2 tsp. curry powder	1 tbsp. cold water
2 tbsp. brown sugar	Whole cloves

Peel, halve and core the apples. Melt the butter in a skillet, then add the curry powder and stir over moderate heat for about 30 seconds. Add 1/2 cup water, brown sugar and lemon juice, then bring to a boil. Add the apple halves and spoon the liquid over the apples. Simmer until apples are just tender, turning occasionally. Remove the apples, then blend the cornstarch and water together and stir into apple liquid. Cook, stirring, until thickened. Return apples to sauce to reheat and coat with sauce. Remove the apples from sauce and stud with cloves, then arrange around the beef ring. Serve the sauce separately.

HAMBURGER PINWHEEL WITH RICE

1 1/2 lb. ground beef	1/3 c. dry bread crumbs
1 egg	2 8-oz. cans tomato sauce with
1/4 c. finely chopped onion	cheese
1/2 tsp. salt	Filling
1/4 tsp. pepper	

Mix the beef with egg, onion, salt, pepper, bread crumbs and 1/2 can tomato sauce and pat out on sheet of foil to about 9 x 10 inches. Spread Filling over beef mixture. Roll as for jelly roll and leave on foil, seam side down. Place in a shallow baking pan. Bake at 350 degrees for 40 minutes, then drain. Pour remaining tomato sauce over beef mixture and bake for 30 minutes longer. 5-6 servings.

Filling

1/4 c. chopped celery	1/4 tsp. poultry seasoning
1/4 c. chopped green pepper	1/2 tsp. salt
2 c. cooked rice	1/8 tsp. pepper

Combine all ingredients in a bowl and mix well.

Mrs. Ann Hoit, Arlington, Texas

RAVIOLI-STUFFED MEAT LOAF

1 1/2 lb. ground beef	1/2 c. dry bread crumbs
1 egg, beaten	1/4 c. milk
3 tbsp. chopped onion	2 15 1/2-oz. cans beef ravioli
1 1/4 tsp. salt	

Preheat oven to 350 degrees. Combine all ingredients except ravioli in a bowl and mix well. Place 1/3 of the beef mixture in a 9 x 5 x 3-inch loaf pan and add 1 can ravioli. Repeat layers, ending with beef mixture and press down firmly. Bake for 1 hour. 6 servings.

Mrs. Betty McDowell, Flagstaff, Arizona

TOP-OF-STOVE MEAT LOAF

1 can tomato soup	1 tsp. salt
1 1/2 lb. ground beef	Dash of pepper
1/2 c. fine bread crumbs	1 tbsp. shortening
1 egg	1/4 c. water
1/3 c. finely chopped onion	1/2 to 1 tsp. horseradish

Mix 1/2 can soup with the beef, bread crumbs, egg, onion, salt and pepper and shape into 2 loaves. Brown in shortening in a skillet, then cover. Cook over low heat for 25 minutes. Drain and top with remaining soup, water and horseradish. Cook for 10 minutes longer. 6 servings.

Mrs. Clara Ennis, Austin, Texas

Cottage Beef Bake (page 94)

casseroles

Ground beef casseroles are a boon to today's busy, cost-conscious homemakers. A pound of ground beef, which is relatively inexpensive, can easily be transformed into a richly flavored casserole with the addition of vegetables, pasta, or sauces. And they are the perfect solution on those in-a-rush days. Simply prepare your casserole the night before or early in the morning. When you come home, just pop it into the oven and relax while it cooks. With a minimum of effort, you will have served your family a nutritious and delicious supper.

From kitchens throughout America's Southland have come favorite ground beef casserole recipes. Why not serve your family one tonight? Just picture how enthusiastically they'll receive Lasagna Loraine, a southern version of the noodles-ground beef-tomato sauce dish that's been a favorite with American families for generations. Or introduce everyone to tortillas, those flat corn pancakes, in Mexican Hot Dish. With tortillas available from your grocer's freezer, this dish is a real time-saver!

The recipes in this section have all been created by southern women — homemakers like you who take enormous pride in serving their families well-cooked, flavorful dishes they have developed themselves. Their pride is reflected in every one of these recipes and will soon be yours to share — when you feature ground beef casseroles at your dinner table!

Parasol Beans (below)

PARASOL BEANS

1 1-lb. can whole Blue Lake green beans	2 tbsp. butter or margarine
1/2 lb. coarsely ground beef	2 tbsp. soy sauce
1 clove of garlic, minced	1 chicken bouillon cube
1/8 tsp. ginger	1 c. thinly sliced onion rings
	2 tbsp. finely chopped parsley

Drain the beans, reserving 1/2 cup liquid. Combine the beef, garlic and ginger in butter in a skillet and cook until browned, stirring to crumble the beef. Reduce heat, then add the reserved bean liquid, soy sauce and bouillon cube and simmer, stirring, until bouillon is dissolved. Add the onion rings, beans and parsley and heat through.

BAKED BEEF AND LIMA BEAN CASSEROLE

1 c. large dried lima beans	2 tbsp. flour
2 tbsp. bacon drippings	1 tsp. salt
1 lb. ground beef	1 tsp. pepper
2 onions, chopped	2 c. canned tomatoes

Place the beans in a saucepan and cover with water. Soak overnight. Add 1 cup water and cook until tender. Heat the bacon drippings in a skillet. Add ground beef and cook until brown, stirring occasionally. Add onions. Stir in the flour, salt and pepper and cook, stirring, for 8 minutes. Place alternate layers of beef mixture, beans and tomatoes in a casserole and add 1 1/2 cups water. Bake at 325 degrees for 2 hours, adding water, if needed. 10 servings.

Mrs. Jack E. Curry, Cromwell, Oklahoma

AMERICAN-ORIENTAL CASSEROLE

3 tbsp. oil	1/4 tsp. pepper
1 lb. ground beef	2 tbsp. soy sauce
1/2 tsp. salt	2 c. diced celery

1 c. diced onion	2 tbsp. milk
1 can cream of mushroom soup	1/2 c. chow mein noodles
1 1-lb. can bean sprouts	

Heat the oil in a saucepan and add the ground beef. Cook until brown. Add the salt, pepper and soy sauce and mix well. Add the celery and onion and cook over low heat until tender. Stir in soup. Drain the bean sprouts and add to beef mixture. Add the milk and mix thoroughly. Pour into a greased 1 1/2-quart casserole and top with chow mein noodles. Bake in 350-degree oven for 40 to 45 minutes. 4-6 servings.

Brenda Bowman, Greenville, Tennessee

BARBECUED HAMBURGER-POTATO CASSEROLE

1 1/2 lb. ground beef	1/2 c. milk
Salt and pepper to taste	1 egg, well beaten
6 med. potatoes, peeled	Barbecue Sauce
1/4 c. butter or margarine	

Brown the ground beef in a skillet and season with salt and pepper. Cook the potatoes in boiling, salted water until done, then drain and mash well. Add the butter and mix. Add milk and egg and beat well. Place alternate layers of potatoes, ground beef and Barbecue Sauce in a casserole, ending with potatoes. Bake at 400 degrees until potatoes are brown.

Barbecue Sauce

1/4 c. vinegar	1/4 tsp. pepper
1 c. water	Dash of red pepper
1 onion, sliced	1/4 c. butter
1 tbsp. sugar	1 tbsp. prepared mustard
1 thick slice lemon	1/2 c. catsup
1 1/2 tsp. salt	3 tbsp. Worcestershire sauce

Combine all ingredients except catsup and Worcestershire sauce in a saucepan and simmer for 30 minutes. Add the catsup and Worcestershire sauce and bring to a boil. Remove from heat.

Nelda W. Bishop, Woodland, Alabama

BEEF-BEAN CASSEROLE

1 1/2 lb. ground beef	1 sm. onion, minced
1/2 c. catsup	1 No. 303 can green lima beans
1/2 tsp. dry mustard	1 No. 303 can red kidney beans
2 tbsp. vinegar	1 No. 303 can pork and beans
3 tbsp. dark brown sugar	1 tsp. salt

Brown the beef in a skillet. Add remaining ingredients and mix well. Place in two 1 1/2-quart casseroles. Bake at 350 degrees for 30 minutes. 12 servings.

Mrs. Eddie Powers, Marston, North Carolina

BEEF AND CARROTS

1 lb. ground beef	1 c. corn flakes
1 sm. onion, chopped	6 carrots
Salt and pepper to taste	1 can cream of celery soup
1 egg, beaten	

Combine the beef, onion, salt, pepper, egg and corn flakes and shape into patties. Place in a shallow baking dish. Broil until brown and drain off fat. Cut carrots into 2-inch pieces and place around the patties. Pour soup over beef mixture and cover with aluminum foil. Bake at 350 degrees until carrots are tender.

Mrs. Henry Mayes, Calhoun, Louisiana

CORNBURGER CASSEROLE

1/2 lb. hamburger	1 egg, well beaten
1 med. onion, diced	1 tsp. salt
1/4 c. chopped celery	1 tsp. paprika
1/3 c. chopped green pepper	1 tsp. melted butter
1 can whole kernel corn	1/4 c. grated cheese
1/2 c. milk	Quartered frankfurters

Combine the hamburger, onion, celery and green pepper in a skillet and cook until brown, stirring frequently. Add the corn, milk, egg, salt, paprika and butter and mix well. Place in a buttered baking dish and sprinkle the cheese on top. Make squares of frankfurters across the cheese. Bake in 350-degree oven for 30 minutes.

Mrs. Fred Disher, Winston-Salem, North Carolina

DUTCH MILL BEEF CASSEROLE

1 lb. ground beef	1 tbsp. soy sauce
1 1/2 c. shredded potatoes	1 c. tomato sauce
1/4 c. finely chopped onion	1 can cheese soup
1/2 c. finely chopped green	1/4 c. sliced stuffed olives
pepper	Parsley
2 tbsp. Worcestershire sauce	

Mix the beef, potatoes, onion, green pepper, Worcestershire sauce and soy sauce and pack 1/2 of the mixture into a 1 1/2-quart casserole. Pour 1/2 cup tomato sauce and 1/2 can cheese soup over beef mixture. Repeat layers. Bake in 350-degree oven for 1 hour and 30 minutes. Garnish with olives and parsley. 6-8 servings.

Mrs. Frank Thomas, Corpus Christi, Texas

CORNY EGGPLANT CASSEROLE

1 med. onion, chopped	1/4 c. milk
Chopped green pepper to taste	2 eggs
2 tsp. sugar	Salt and pepper to taste
1 c. ground beef	1 1/2 slices dry toast,
Corn oil	crumbled
1 c. cooked drained eggplant	4 crackers, crushed
2 c. cream-style corn	1/2 c. grated cheese

Cook the onion, green pepper, 1 teaspoon sugar and beef in small amount of oil in a skillet until brown. Add the eggplant, corn, milk, eggs, remaining sugar, salt, pepper and 1 slice toast and mix. Add the crackers and 1 tablespoon corn oil and mix well. Turn into a baking dish and sprinkle cheese and remaining toast over top. Place baking dish in a pan of hot water. Bake at 350 degrees for about 30 minutes.

Mrs. A. J. Frazier, Llano, Texas

EGGPLANT CASSEROLE

3 tbsp. butter	1 c. tomato sauce
1 lb. lean ground beef	1 c. water
1 med. onion, finely chopped	Salt and pepper to taste
1/4 c. pine nuts	1 med. eggplant

Combine all ingredients except eggplant in a skillet and simmer for 15 minutes. Peel the eggplant and slice 1/4 inch thick. Place 1/3 of the eggplant in an 8 x 10-inch casserole, then add half the beef mixture. Repeat layers, ending with eggplant. Cover. Bake at 325 degrees for 30 minutes or until eggplant is tender. 6 servings.

Mrs. Carmen Kazen Ferris, Austin, Texas

ITALIAN EGGPLANT CASSEROLE

1 med. eggplant	1 green pepper, chopped
Milk	Salt and pepper to taste
1 egg, beaten	2 cans tomato sauce
Flour	1 pkg. sliced mozzarella cheese
1 lb. ground beef	1/2 c. grated cheese
1 onion, chopped	Oregano to taste

Peel and slice the eggplant. Dip slices in milk, then in egg. Dip in flour. Cook in small amount of fat in a skillet until brown. Remove from skillet and drain. Cook the beef, onion, green pepper, salt and pepper in same skillet until brown. Add the tomato sauce and mix. Place alternate layers of eggplant, beef mixture and cheese slices in a casserole. Sprinkle with grated cheese and oregano. Bake at 350 degrees until cheese is melted. 4-5 servings.

Mrs. Priscilla J. Pruitt, Jacksonville, North Carolina

Stuffed Cabbage Rolls (below)

STUFFED CABBAGE ROLLS

1/2 c. finely chopped onion	1/8 tsp. basil
5 slices bacon, chopped	6 lge. cabbage leaves
3 c. bite-sized shredded	1/2 c. sour cream
rice biscuits, crushed	1 tbsp. flour
1 lb. lean ground beef	1 can tomato soup
1 tsp. salt	1/4 c. (packed) shredded
1/4 tsp. pepper	sharp cheese

Preheat the oven to 350 degrees. Brown the onion and bacon together and drain. Combine 2/3 cup cereal crumbs, ground beef, bacon mixture, salt, pepper and basil, then mix well. Pour boiling water over the cabbage leaves and allow to stand for 2 to 3 minutes, then drain. Divide the beef mixture among the cabbage leaves, then roll and fasten with toothpicks. Place in a baking dish. Mix the sour cream with flour, then add the soup. Pour over the cabbage rolls and cover. Bake for 30 minutes or until bubbly. Combine the cheese and remaining cereal crumbs, and sprinkle on rolls. Bake, uncovered, for 20 minutes longer or until browned. 6 servings.

RUTABAGA CASSEROLE

1 lb. ground beef	1 No. 303 can diced rutabagas,
Salt and pepper to taste	drained
1 tbsp. flour	1 can English peas
2 c. milk	3 to 4 c. whipped potatoes

Season the beef with salt and pepper, then shape into small balls. Brown in small amount of fat, then place in a 2-quart casserole. Add flour to the pan drippings, stirring to blend, then add milk, stirring until thickened and smooth. Season with salt and pepper. Place the rutabagas and peas over the meatballs, then add the gravy and mix lightly. Top with whipped potatoes. Bake at 450 degrees about 30 minutes.

Mrs. Weldon Johnson, Cookville, Texas

RAISIN MEXICALI TAMALE CASSEROLE

1 lb. lean ground beef	1 tsp. salt
1 tbsp. vegetable oil	2 tsp. chili powder
1 sm. onion, chopped	1/3 c. cornmeal
1 clove of garlic, pressed	1 c. pitted ripe olives
1 No. 2 can tomatoes	Tamale Topping
1 No. 2 can cream-style corn	3/4 c. grated sharp Cheddar
1/2 c. dark seedless raisins	cheese

Cook the beef in oil until partially done, then add the onion and garlic. Cook until onion is transparent. Add the tomatoes, corn, raisins and seasonings and simmer for 15 minutes. Stir in the cornmeal slowly and cook, stirring until thickened. Add the olives, then turn into a 2-quart baking dish. Cover with Tamale Topping and sprinkle with cheese. Bake at 400 degrees for about 15 minutes.

Tamale Topping

1/2 c. cornmeal	2 tbsp. butter or margarine
1/2 tsp. salt	

Stir the cornmeal into 1 cup cold water, then stir into 2 1/2 cups boiling water. Add the salt and butter and cook until thick, stirring frequently.

Raisin Mexicali Tamale Casserole (above)

BEEF AND HOMINY

2 tbsp. shortening	1 tbsp. chili powder
1 onion, chopped	1 can hominy
1 lb. ground beef	1/2 c. sliced stuffed olives
1/2 c. tomato juice or catsup	1 c. shredded American cheese
1 tsp. salt	Paprika

Melt the shortening in a heavy skillet. Add the onion and beef and cook, stirring, until beef loses red color. Add the tomato juice, salt, chili powder, undrained hominy and olives and cover. Cook over low heat for 20 minutes. Spread cheese over top and sprinkle with paprika. Cover and cook for 5 minutes longer or until cheese is melted.

Mrs. Fred E. Hicks, Knoxville, Tennessee

HOMINY CASSEROLE

1 lb. ground beef	1 15 1/2-oz. can tamales
1 onion, chopped fine	1 4 1/2-oz. can pitted ripe
1 tsp. salt	olives
Pepper to taste	1 can cream of chicken soup
1 No. 2 1/2 can hominy	

Cook the ground beef and onion with salt and pepper in a skillet until brown. Drain the hominy and add to ground beef mixture. Chop the tamales and olives and add to ground beef mixture. Add the soup and mix well. Pour into a 2-quart casserole. Bake at 350 degrees for 30 minutes. 6 servings.

Mrs. John Vachon, Beaumont, Texas

HOMINY AND GROUND BEEF

1 1/2 lb. ground beef	1/2 tsp. pepper
1 lge. onion, chopped fine	1 tbsp. chili powder
2 1/2 c. cooked hominy	2 c. canned tomatoes
4 tbsp. margarine	1/2 c. grated cheese
1 tsp. salt	

Brown the beef, onion and hominy in margarine in a skillet, then stir in seasonings. Add the tomatoes and bring to a boil. Cook until thick. Place in a greased casserole and sprinkle with cheese. Bake in 350-degree oven for about 30 minutes. 6 servings.

Mrs. R. D. Smallwood, Worthington, West Virginia

VEGETABLE-MEAT CASSEROLE

1 lb. hamburger	1 sm. onion, chopped
1/2 tsp. salt	1 can tomato soup
Dash of pepper	1 soup can water

8 med. potatoes, sliced
1 15-oz. can peas, drained

Fine bread crumbs

Mix the hamburger with salt, pepper and onion and cook in a skillet until brown. Mix the tomato soup with water and mix with hamburger mixture. Heat through. Place alternate layers of potatoes, peas and hamburger mixture in a greased 2-quart casserole and top with bread crumbs. Cover. Bake at 350 degrees for 1 hour and 30 minutes. 8 servings.

Mrs. Carrie Ryland, Durham, North Carolina

HONG KONG HAMBURGER

2 tbsp. shortening
1 sm. onion, chopped
1 lb. ground beef, crumbled
6 eggs

1 tsp. salt
1/4 tsp. pepper
1 1-lb. can bean sprouts

Melt the shortening in a frypan. Add the onion and cook, stirring frequently, until tender but not brown. Stir in the beef and cook until browned. Place the eggs in a large bowl and add salt and pepper. Beat with a rotary beater or electric mixer until light. Drain the bean sprouts and stir into the eggs. Stir in the beef mixture and place in a 13 x 9 x 2-inch greased baking pan. Bake at 350 degrees for 30 minutes or until puffed and golden. Serve with soy sauce, if desired. 6-8 servings.

Mrs. Clark Dow, Enid, Oklahoma

CHEESE-SPAGHETTI CASSEROLE

1 lb. ground beef
2 c. tomato sauce
3 c. water
2 1 1/2-oz. packages
   spaghetti sauce mix
1 1/2 tsp. salt
1 1-lb. package spaghetti

1/4 c. butter
5 tbsp. flour
2 c. milk
1 1/2 c. shredded process
   American cheese
1/4 c. grated Parmesan cheese

Brown the beef in a large saucepan, then drain. Add the tomato sauce, water, spaghetti sauce mix and 1/2 teaspoon salt. Simmer, uncovered, stirring frequently, for 30 minutes. Break the spaghetti into thirds and cook according to package directions, rinsing and draining well. Melt the butter in a saucepan, then stir in flour and remaining salt. Add the milk slowly and cook, stirring constantly, over medium heat until thickened. Add 1 cup American cheese and Parmesan cheese and stir until melted. Arrange alternate layers of spaghetti, beef sauce and cheese sauce in two 12 x 7 1/2 x 2-inch casseroles. Sprinkle top with remaining cheese. Bake at 350 degrees for 15 to 20 minutes or until bubbly. Serve at once.

Mrs. Cecil R. Randolph, Dallas, Texas

HAMBURGER-SPAGHETTI DINNER

1 12-oz. package spaghetti
1/2 med. onion, chopped
Shortening
1 1/2 lb. hamburger

1 can cream of mushroom soup
1 15-oz. can tomato sauce
1/2 c. chopped ripe olives
1 c. shredded cheese

Cook the spaghetti according to package directions and drain. Brown the onion lightly in small amount of shortening. Add the hamburger and cook, covered, until done. Combine the soup with tomato sauce and olives and mix thoroughly. Add to hamburger mixture, then stir in the spaghetti. Place in a baking dish. Cover with cheese. Bake at 350 degrees for 15 minutes. 8 servings.

Mrs. Edna Crow, Hollis, Oklahoma

MORE CASSEROLE

1 8-oz. package spaghetti
1 lb. ground beef
2 tbsp. onion puree
2 tbsp. garlic puree
1 tbsp. corn oil
1 No. 2 can solid-pack tomatoes
1 c. water
3 tbsp. chili powder

1 4-oz. can mushroom pieces
1 pkg. frozen English peas,
   cooked
1 can whole kernel corn
1 tsp. pepper
1 tsp. salt
2 c. grated sharp cheese

Cook the spaghetti according to package directions and drain. Brown the ground beef, onion and garlic in oil, then add the tomatoes, water and chili powder. Cover; simmer for 30 minutes. Combine the mushrooms, peas, corn, pepper and salt. Blend in the spaghetti. Fill a large greased casserole with half the beef mixture, then half the spaghetti mixture. Repeat layers. Sprinkle the top with cheese. Bake for 30 minutes in a 350-degree oven. 8 servings.

Mrs. Joel R. Bond, Terrell, Texas

MYSTICAL CASSEROLE

1 lb. ground beef
1/2 c. dry bread crumbs
1/8 tsp. pepper
1/2 tsp. chili powder
1 egg
1/2 c. unsweetened applesauce
1 tsp. salt
1/8 tsp. sage

Dash of garlic salt
Flour
1 sm. green pepper, chopped
1 stalk celery, chopped
1 sm. onion, thinly sliced
1 carrot, thinly sliced
1 c. tomato juice

Combine the first 9 ingredients and mix well. Shape into walnut-sized balls, then dredge in flour. Brown in a small amount fat and place in a casserole. Combine the green pepper, celery, onion and carrot, then sprinkle over the meatballs. Pour the tomato juice over the top. Bake in a 300-degree oven for 1 hour.

Mrs. Barbara Rawdoi. ?rants, New Mexico

MEXICAN TORTILLA CASSEROLE

1 lb. ground beef	1 sm. can green chilies,
1 pkg. tortillas	chopped
1 lb. cheese, grated	1 sm. can taco sauce
1 med. onion, finely chopped	1/2 lge. can evaporated milk
1 can cream of chicken soup	2 1/2 c. water
1 can cream of mushroom soup	

Brown the beef in a skillet. Break tortillas in small pieces. Place alternate layers of tortillas, beef, cheese and onion in a large baking dish. Mix remaining ingredients and pour over onion. Bake at 350 degrees for 30 minutes. 8-10 servings.

Mrs. Ewell Mote, Tulia, Texas

MEATBALLS AND VEGETABLES

1 lb. ground beef	2 tbsp. butter
1/2 c. fine dry bread crumbs	1 can cream of mushroom soup
1/3 c. milk	1 1/2 c. shredded Cheddar
1 egg, beaten	cheese
1/4 c. finely chopped onion	1/2 tsp. rubbed sage
1 tsp. salt	2 10-oz. packages frozen
1/4 tsp. dry mustard	mixed vegetables

Preheat oven to 350 degrees. Combine the beef, bread crumbs, milk, egg, onion, salt and mustard in a bowl and mix lightly. Shape into twenty-four 1 1/2-inch balls. Melt the butter in a large skillet and brown the meatballs slowly on all sides. Combine the soup, cheese and sage. Cook the vegetables according to package directions and drain. Arrange the meatballs around sides of a shallow 1 1/2-quart casserole, then spoon the soup mixture into center and arrange vegetables over the soup mixture. Cover with foil. Bake for 30 minutes. 6 servings.

Meatballs and Vegetables (above)

MEXICAN HOT DISH

2 lb. hamburger	1 can cream of mushroom soup
1/2 lge. onion, chopped	1 can cream of chicken soup
Salt and pepper to taste	1 doz. tortillas
Dash of garlic powder	1 lb. longhorn cheese, grated
1 9-oz. can taco sauce	

Cook the hamburger and onion with seasonings until brown, then drain off excess fat. Add the taco sauce and soups and mix well. Line an 8 x 14-inch pan with foil, leaving enough on ends to fold back over pan. Break 4 tortillas into small pieces and place in pan. Pour 1/2 of hamburger mixture over tortillas, then top with 4 more broken tortillas and 1/2 of the cheese. Add the remaining hamburger mixture and top with remaining broken tortillas. Sprinkle remaining cheese over top. Fold foil back over pan. Bake for 30 to 40 minutes in 350-degree oven. 10-12 servings.

Mrs. Nell Berry, Monahans, Texas

WEST OF THE PECOS ENCHILADAS

1 lb. lean ground beef	1 6-oz. can tomato paste
1 tsp. salt	1 10 1/2-oz. can tomato soup
1/2 lb. longhorn cheese, grated	2 c. water
1 can chopped ripe olives	1/2 c. cooking oil
1 c. chopped onions	2 tbsp. chili powder
2 8-oz. cans tomato sauce	1 tsp. garlic powder
	1 doz. tortillas

Cook the ground beef, stirring frequently, until browned, then add 1/2 teaspoon salt. Reserve 1 cup cheese. Add the remaining cheese, olives and onions to beef mixture and mix well. Combine the tomato sauce, tomato paste, soup, water, oil, chili powder, garlic powder and remaining salt and bring to a boil. Simmer for several minutes. Dip the tortillas into the sauce and place on a plate. Place a heaping tablespoon of the beef mixture in center of each tortilla and roll. Place filled tortillas close together in baking dish and pour 1 cup sauce over tortillas. Bake at 350 degrees for 15 minutes or until heated through. Sprinkle with reserved cheese and bake until cheese is melted. Serve tortillas with remaining sauce. 4 servings.

Mrs. Louise Cox, Pecos, Texas

OLD-TIMER FAVORITE CASSEROLE

1 lb. dried blackeye peas	1 c. catsup
1 lb. ground beef	6 slices bread
1 lge. onion, chopped	

Cook the peas according to package directions, then drain and reserve 1/2 cup liquid. Brown the beef lightly, then drain off excess fat. Place half the peas, half the beef and half the onion and half the catsup in layers in a 2-quart casserole. Place 3 slices bread over top, then repeat the peas, beef, onion and bread layers. Combine the remaining catsup with the reserved liquid, then pour over the top. Bake at 350 degrees for 1 hour.

Mrs. Sarah Mills, Spartanburg, South Carolina

Meatballs Baked in Mushroom Sauce (below)

MEATBALLS BAKED IN MUSHROOM SAUCE

1 lb. ground beef	1 egg, lightly beaten
1/2 lb. ground pork	1 tsp. salt
1 c. instant nonfat dry milk	1/4 tsp. pepper
1 1/2 c. soft bread crumbs	1/2 c. water
1/4 c. chopped onion	Mushroom Sauce

Combine all the ingredients except the Mushroom Sauce and mix thoroughly. Shape into balls and place in a baking dish. Bake at 350 degrees for 40 minutes. Pour the Mushroom Sauce over the meatballs and bake for 20 minutes longer, basting once during baking.

Mushroom Sauce

1/4 c. butter	2 c. broth or bouillon
1/2 lb. sliced fresh mushrooms	1/4 c. sour cream
1/4 c. chopped onion	1/2 tsp. salt
1/4 c. flour	Paprika to taste
1/2 c. instant nonfat dry milk	

Melt the butter in a 1 1/2-quart saucepan, then add the mushrooms and onion. Saute for 5 minutes. Remove the mushrooms and onion from the butter and remove the pan from the heat. Add the flour and nonfat dry milk and mix well. Stir in the broth gradually and cook until thick, stirring until smooth. Stir in the sour cream, seasonings and mushroom mixture.

Salisbury Sauerbraten (below)

SALISBURY SAUERBRATEN

1 can beef gravy	1/2 tsp. ground ginger
1 lb. ground beef	1 1-lb. can sm. whole
1/3 c. fine dry bread	potatoes
crumbs	4 gingersnaps, finely crushed
2 tbsp. chopped onion	1 tbsp. brown sugar
1/2 tsp. grated lemon rind	1 tbsp. wine vinegar

Combine 1/3 cup of the gravy, beef, crumbs, onion, lemon rind and ginger and mix thoroughly. Shape into 4 patties and place in a 10 x 6 x 2-inch baking dish. Bake at 350 degrees for 20 minutes. Spoon off fat. Drain the potatoes and arrange around patties. Combine the remaining gravy, gingersnaps, brown sugar and vinegar and pour over the patties and potatoes. Bake, covered, for 20 minutes longer. 4 servings.

ARCADIA CASSEROLE

1 1/2 lb. ground beef	Salt to taste
1 med. onion, chopped	3 beef bouillon cubes
3 tbsp. oil	1 1/2 c. rice
1/2 c. catsup	Buttered bread crumbs
1 can tomato soup	

Brown the beef and onion in oil, then add the catsup, soup and salt. Dissolve the bouillon in 3 cups boiling water, then stir in the rice and cook until tender. Place the rice in a buttered baking dish, then spread the beef mixture over top. Cover with bread crumbs. Bake at 350 degrees until golden brown.

Mrs. Charles Hyatt, Roebuck, South Carolina

CABBAGE ROLLS WITH SOUR CREAM SAUCE

2 c. seasoned ground beef	1 egg, well beaten
1/4 c. diced onion	6 lge. cabbage leaves
1/2 c. diced celery	1/2 c. tomato puree
1 c. cooked rice	1/2 c. water
1 tbsp. prepared mustard	1 c. sour cream

Preheat oven to 350 degrees. Brown the beef and onion in 2 tablespoons fat in large skillet over low heat. Remove from heat and stir in the celery, rice, mustard and egg. Cook cabbage leaves for 3 minutes in boiling salted water, then drain. Place the beef mixture in cabbage leaves, then roll and fasten with toothpicks. Place close together in greased 11 1/2 x 7 1/2-inch baking dish and pour tomato puree and water over cabbage rolls. Bake, covered, for 30 minutes. Remove the cabbage rolls, then stir the sour cream into pan liquid and serve over cabbage rolls. 6 servings.

Mrs. Martha Hall, Lexington, Kentucky

BEEF-KRAUT CASSEROLE

1 1/2 lb. ground beef	Salt and pepper
1 1/2 c. rice	1 No. 3 can sauerkraut, drained
1 med. onion, chopped	

Combine the beef, rice, onion, salt and pepper and mix thoroughly. Arrange alternate layers of the beef mixture and sauerkraut in casserole. Add water to cover. Bake at 350 degrees for 1 hour and 30 minutes. 6-8 servings.

Mrs. Ann Sims, Mobile, Alabama

ARROZ CON CARNE

1 c. rice	1 tsp. salt
1 lb. ground beef	1 can tomato soup
2 sm. onions, chopped	1 c. water
1 green pepper, chopped	1/2 c. vinegar
3 cloves	2 tbsp. sugar
1 bay leaf	

Cook the rice according to package directions and drain. Cook the ground beef, onions, green pepper, cloves, bay leaf and salt in a skillet until browned, then remove the cloves and bay leaf. Stir in the soup, water, vinegar, sugar and rice and place in a baking dish. Bake at 350 degrees until heated through.

Mrs. Carl Morris, Princeton, Kentucky

CABBAGE AND RICE GUMPIES

1 c. cooked rice	Dash of garlic powder
1 lb. hamburger	1 1-lb. can tomato sauce
1/2 tsp. poultry seasoning	1 med. cabbage
1/4 tsp. salt	

Mix the rice, hamburger and seasonings in a bowl and stir in 1/2 can tomato sauce. Separate cabbage leaves and place 2 layers of leaves in a 2-quart casserole. Spoon hamburger mixture in nests in cabbage leaves. Repeat until all ingredients are used and pour remaining tomato sauce over top. Cover. Bake at 350 degrees for 1 hour. 4-6 servings.

Mrs. Lorenzo Michand, Tallahassee, Florida

FAMILY CASSEROLE

1 med. onion, finely chopped	1 tsp. curry powder
1 lb. ground beef	1 tsp. onion salt
2 1/4 c. cooked rice	1 tsp. salt
1 No. 2 can tomatoes	1/8 tsp. pepper
3 tbsp. soy sauce	3 strips bacon
1 tbsp. Worcestershire sauce	

Cook onion in 1 tablespoon hot fat until slightly browned. Add the ground beef and brown lightly. Mix with the rice, tomatoes and seasonings. Place in a 1 1/2-quart casserole and top with bacon. Bake at 375 degrees for about 30 minutes or until bacon is crisp. 4-6 servings.

Brenda Willingham, Tahlequah, Oklahoma

GROUND BEEF ORIENTAL

2 onions, chopped	1 1/2 c. water
1 c. sliced celery	2 to 4 tbsp. soy sauce
3 tbsp. melted butter	1/4 tsp. pepper
1/2 c. rice, cooked	1 1-lb. can bean sprouts,
1 lb. ground beef	drained
1 can cream of chicken soup	1 can Chinese noodles
1 can cream of mushroom soup	

Brown the onions and celery in butter, then remove from pan and brown the rice and ground beef. Combine the soups, water, soy sauce and pepper in buttered 2-quart casserole. Add the onion mixture, beef mixture and bean sprouts and stir lightly to blend. Bake, covered, at 350 degrees for 30 minutes. Uncover and bake for 30 minutes longer. Serve with warm Chinese noodles.

Alice F. Mavis, Clovis, New Mexico

ORIENTAL CASSEROLE

1 1/2 lb. ground chuck	2/3 c. rice
1 sm. onion, chopped	1 tsp. salt
1/2 c. chopped celery	1 tsp. pepper
1 can water chestnuts	1/3 c. soy sauce
1 sm. can mushrooms	

Brown the ground chuck, onion and celery in a skillet. Drain the water chestnuts and mushrooms and reserve liquid. Add the water chestnuts, mushrooms, rice, salt, pepper and soy sauce to ground chuck mixture. Add enough water to reserved liquid to make 2 cups liquid and stir into the ground chuck mixture. Cover. Bake at 350 degrees for 1 hour. 6-8 servings.

Mrs. Frances Harwell, Opelika, Alabama

POOR BOY CASSEROLE SUPPER

1 1/2 lb. hamburger	1 1/2 tsp. salt
1 sm. potato, grated	1/8 tsp. pepper
1 sm. onion, grated	2 tbsp. shortening
1/2 carrot, grated	1 can cream of mushroom soup
1/2 c. dry bread crumbs	1 soup can milk
1 egg	1/2 c. instant rice

Combine the beef, vegetables and bread crumbs, then add the egg, salt and pepper and mix until well blended. Shape into meatballs. Brown in the shortening over medium heat. Combine the soup, milk and rice in a casserole and add the meatballs. Cover. Bake at 350 degrees for 30 minutes. 6-8 servings.

Bettye Sandridge, Evening Shade, Arkansas

RICE JAMBOREE

1 c. chopped onions	2 1/2 c. tomatoes
2 tbsp. shortening	2 1/2 c. rice
1 lb. ground beef	2 c. oven-toasted rice cereal
1 tsp. salt	1 1/2 tsp. melted butter or
1/4 tsp. pepper	margarine
1 8-oz. can peas	

Cook the onions in hot shortening until lightly browned. Add the beef and seasonings and cook until beef is browned. Drain the peas and reserve 1/4 cup liquid, then add the peas, reserved liquid, tomatoes and rice to beef mixture, stirring lightly. Place in greased 2-quart casserole and cover. Bake in 325-degree oven for about 45 minutes. Remove cover and sprinkle top with finely crushed cereal mixed with butter. Return to oven, uncovered, and bake for 15 minutes longer. 8 servings.

Della Worford, Irvine, Kentucky

Mexibeef (below)

MEXIBEEF

1/4 c. butter	1/8 tsp. pepper
1 c. chopped onion	1 c. milk
1 lb. ground beef	1/2 c. sliced black ripe
1 tbsp. flour	olives
1 1/2 tsp. chili powder	1 c. shredded Cheddar cheese
1 tsp. salt	3 c. hot cooked rice

Melt the butter in a frypan, then add the onion and beef. Cook until the onion is transparent and beef crumbly. Blend in the flour, chili powder, salt and pepper, then stir in the milk. Cook, stirring, until the sauce is thickened. Add the olives. Fold 1/2 of the cheese into the rice, then spoon over bottom and into a border around sides of a shallow 1 1/2-quart casserole. Fill center with the beef mixture. Sprinkle with remaining cheese. Bake at 350 degrees for 20 to 25 minutes or until heated through. Garnish with green pepper rings, if desired. 6 servings.

SQUASH CASSEROLE

1 lb. ground lean beef	1 tsp. salt
1 c. rice, washed	1/2 tsp. basil
1 sm. green pepper, chopped	4 lge. yellow summer squash,
1 onion, chopped	sliced
1/4 c. salad oil	Grated cheese
1 No. 2 1/2 can tomatoes	Dash of paprika

Brown the beef, rice, green pepper and onion in oil in a heavy skillet, then add tomatoes, salt and basil. Place the squash in a casserole and top with beef mixture. Cover. Bake at 350 degrees for about 30 minutes, stirring once. Top with grated cheese and paprika. Return to oven for 15 to 20 minutes longer or until done. 4-6 servings.

Mrs. Cephas Brainerd, Hot Springs, Arkansas

AMERICAN RAVIOLI

2 tbsp. shortening	1 can cream of mushroom soup
1 med. onion, finely chopped	1 lb. Cheddar cheese, grated
1 lb. ground beef	1 lge. can tomato sauce
1 pkg. long macaroni	1/2 tomato sauce can water

Melt the shortening in skillet and saute the onion in shortening until tender. Add the ground beef and cook until browned. Cook macaroni according to package directions. Place half the beef mixture in a casserole and add half the macaroni. Add half the soup, then add half the cheese. Repeat layers. Mix the tomato sauce and water and pour over the cheese. Bake at 425 degrees for 30 minutes or until cheese is melted. 6-8 servings.

Mrs. Mary Nan Marek, Alice, Texas

CATTLE RUSTLER'S HASH

1 sm. package macaroni	1 8-oz. can tomato sauce
1 lb. lean ground beef	1/2 lb. grated Cheddar cheese
1/4 c. finely cut onion (opt.)	1 can cream of mushroom or
2 tbsp. chili blend	chicken soup
1 tsp. salt	

Cook the macaroni according to package directions and drain. Brown the beef in an ovenproof skillet, then push to one side and add the onion. Cook until limp but not brown. Add the chili blend, salt and tomato sauce and mix well. Cover skillet and simmer for 20 minutes. Add the macaroni to the beef mixture, then top with the cheese. Spread the soup over the top. Bake at 375 degrees for 30 to 40 minutes. 6 servings.

Mrs. William S. Bevers, Post, Texas

COMPANY BEEF CASSEROLE

1 lb. ground beef	1/4 c. chopped green pepper
2 tbsp. shortening or butter	2 tbsp. chopped parsley
1 med. onion, chopped	5 oz. elbow macaroni
2 c. canned tomatoes	Salt and pepper to taste
1 tbsp. catsup	1 can cream of mushroom soup
1 tbsp. steak sauce	1 c. grated cheese

Brown the ground beef in shortening in heavy skillet then add the onion, tomatoes, catsup, steak sauce, green pepper and parsley. Simmer for 30 minutes. Cook the macaroni according to package directions and drain. Combine the macaroni and ground beef mixture in a baking dish, then season with salt and pepper. Spoon soup into mixture and mix lightly, lifting from bottom. Sprinkle cheese over top. Bake in a 350-degree oven for 30 minutes until top is bubbly and brown. 8-10 servings.

Mrs. Marie Cole, Grantville, Georgia

COTTAGE BEEF BAKE

1 7-oz. package elbow macaroni	1 tbsp. flour
2 c. creamed cottage cheese	2 tsp. Italian seasoning
1 med. onion, chopped	1 8-oz. can tomato sauce
2 tbsp. butter	2 c. shredded process American cheese
1 lb. lean ground beef	
1 tsp. salt	Buttered bread crumbs

Cook the macaroni according to package directions and drain. Combine with the cottage cheese and set aside. Saute the onion in butter until transparent. Add the ground beef and cook until lightly browned. Stir in the salt, flour, Italian seasoning and tomato sauce and cook for 1 minute. Pour 1/3 of the beef mixture into a buttered 2-quart casserole. Top with 1/2 of the macaroni mixture, then 1/2 of the shredded cheese. Repeat layers, ending with beef mixture. Sprinkle buttered bread crumbs over top. Bake, uncovered, at 325 degrees for 45 minutes. Garnish edge with additional grated cheese and parsley. Let stand for 10 minutes before serving. 6-8 servings.

Photograph for this recipe on page 74.

HACIENDA CASSEROLE

1 1/2 lb. ground beef chuck	1 No. 303 can whole kernel corn
Cooking oil	2 cans tomato sauce
2 onions, chopped	Salt and pepper to taste
1 green pepper, diced	1/2 c. bread crumbs
1 c. diced celery	1/2 c. grated Cheddar cheese
2 c. cooked macaroni	
6 hard-boiled eggs, sliced	

Brown the beef in small amount of oil. Mix the onions, green pepper and celery. Arrange half the beef mixture in a greased 2-quart casserole, then top with half the macaroni. Place half the onion mixture, eggs and corn over macaroni. Arrange the remaining onion mixture, macaroni, corn and beef in casserole. Pour tomato sauce over all, adding water, if needed to come to edge of the beef. Season with salt and pepper. Top with bread crumbs, then cheese. Bake at 350 degrees for 30 minutes or until bubbly. 8-10 servings.

Mrs. J. W. Eisenhauer, Siloam Springs, Arkansas

HAMBURGER-PECAN CASSEROLE

1 1/2 lb. hamburger	2 soup cans water
Salt and pepper to taste	1 1/2 c. shell macaroni
1/4 c. chopped onion	1 4-oz. can mushrooms
1/2 c. diced American cheese	1/2 c. chopped pecans
1 can cream of mushroom soup	Crushed round buttery crackers
1 can tomato soup	

Combine the hamburger, salt, pepper and onion in skillet and saute until lightly browned. Add the cheese, soups, water and macaroni and simmer for 20 minutes or until macaroni is tender. Add the mushrooms, pecans and additional water if needed. Pour into buttered baking dish and top with crushed crackers. Bake at 300 degrees for 1 hour. 8 servings.

Alice Black, Lafayette, Louisiana

ITALIAN DELIGHT

2 lb. lean ground beef	1 c. grated sharp cheese
2 tbsp. butter	1 tbsp. brown sugar
3 med. onions, diced	1 sm. jar stuffed olives,
1 green pepper, diced	sliced
2 cans tomato sauce	1 tsp. pepper
2 garlic buds, minced	1 tsp. salt
1 tbsp. Worcestershire sauce	1 8-oz. package shell
1 can whole kernel corn	macaroni
1 med. can mushrooms	

Brown the beef in the butter, then add the onions and green pepper and saute lightly. Add the remaining ingredients except the macaroni and simmer for 5 minutes. Cook the macaroni according to package direction, then rinse in cold water. Mix with the beef mixture and place in a casserole. Bake for 1 hour in 350-degree oven. 8-10 servings.

Beatrice Ware, St. Petersburg, Florida

INSIDE-OUT RAVIOLI CASSEROLE

1 7-oz. package macaroni	1 6-oz. can tomato paste
1 lb. ground beef	1 1-lb. can spaghetti sauce
1 med. onion, chopped	with mushrooms
1 clove of garlic, minced	1/2 tsp. salt
Salad oil	Dash of pepper
1 10-oz. package frozen	1 c. shredded sharp cheese
chopped spinach	1/2 c. soft bread crumbs
1 8-oz. can tomato sauce	2 eggs, well beaten

Cook the macaroni according to package directions and drain. Brown the beef, onion and garlic in 1 tablespoon oil. Cook the spinach according to package directions, then drain and reserve the liquid. Add water to the reserved liquid to measure 1 cup, then add to the beef mixture. Stir in the tomato sauce, tomato paste, spaghetti sauce, salt and pepper and simmer for 10 minutes. Combine the spinach, macaroni, cheese, crumbs, eggs and 1/4 cup oil, then spread in a 13 x 9 x 2-inch baking dish. Top with the beef sauce. Bake at 350 degrees for 30 minutes. Allow to stand 10 minutes before serving. 8-10 servings.

Mary Perry, La Grange, Georgia

MOCK RAVIOLI

1 lb. shell macaroni	**1 clove of garlic, chopped**
1/2 c. salad oil	**1 tsp. sage**
1/2 c. minced dried parsley	**1 tsp. salt**
1/2 c. cooked chopped spinach	**Beef Sauce**
1 c. soft bread crumbs	**1/2 c. grated Parmesan or**
4 eggs, well beaten	**Romano cheese**

Cook the macaroni according to package directions and drain. Combine remaining ingredients except the Beef Sauce and cheese. Place layers of macaroni, spinach mixture and Beef Sauce in a large greased casserole, then repeat layers, ending with the sauce. Sprinkle with cheese. Bake at 350 degrees for 30 minutes.

Beef Sauce

2 onions, chopped	**1 can tomato sauce**
1 clove of garlic, chopped	**1 can tomato paste**
2 tbsp. salad oil	**1 1/2 c. water**
2 lb. ground beef	**1/2 tsp. Italian herb mix**
1 4-oz. can mushrooms, drained	**Salt to taste**

Brown the onions and garlic in oil slightly, then add the ground beef and cook until crumbly. Add the remaining ingredients and simmer for 2 hours.

Mrs. Hilda Stokes, Lakeland, Florida

HAMBURGER CASSEROLE

1 lb. hamburger	**1 can macaroni and cheese**
1 med. onion	**1 tsp. salt**
1 carton sour cream	**Pepper to taste**
1 8-oz. package cream cheese	

Brown the hamburger and onion until onion is soft, then drain off excess fat. Blend sour cream and cream cheese together in a skillet and melt cream cheese, stirring constantly, over low heat. Place the macaroni in a casserole and top with the hamburger mixture. Pour the sour cream mixture over top. Season with salt and pepper. Bake in a 350-degree oven for about 40 minutes or until bubbly.

Mrs. H. E. Dalton, Douglasville, Georgia

SPANISH MACARONI

1 c. macaroni	**1/2 tsp. salt**
1 med. onion, chopped	**Dash of pepper**
1/2 green pepper, chopped	**1 can tomato soup**
1 tbsp. margarine	**1/4 lb. cheese, cut into pieces**
1/2 lb. ground beef	**Bread crumbs**

Cook the macaroni according to package directions and drain. Saute the onion and green pepper in margarine, then add the ground beef, salt and pepper. Cook until lightly browned. Add the soup and cheese. Combine the beef mixture with the macaroni and place in a 1-quart baking dish. Top with bread crumbs. Bake at 350 degrees for 25 to 30 minutes. 4 servings.

Alice Corman, Oxford, Mississippi

ALL-AMERICAN MACARONI CASSEROLE

1 1/2 lb. ground beef	3/4 tsp. oregano leaves
2 med. onions, chopped	1/4 tsp. crushed red pepper
1 med. green pepper, diced	3 qt. boiling water
1 6-oz. can tomato paste	2 c. elbow macaroni
2 8-oz. cans tomato sauce	1 c. creamed cottage cheese
Salt	1 c. grated Cheddar cheese

Cook the ground beef in a large saucepan until brown, stirring frequently, then drain off fat. Add the onions and green pepper and cook for 1 minute. Stir in the tomato paste, tomato sauce, 1 1/2 teaspoons salt, oregano and red pepper and cover. Cook over low heat for 45 minutes. Add 1 tablespoon salt to boiling water, then add macaroni gradually so that water continues to boil. Cook, stirring occasionally, until tender. Drain in a colander. Place half the macaroni in a 2 1/2-quart casserole and add half the beef mixture. Spoon cottage cheese over beef mixture and sprinkle with 1/4 cup Cheddar cheese. Repeat layers of remaining macaroni, beef sauce and Cheddar cheese. Bake in 375-degree oven for 15 minutes. Cover loosely with foil and bake for 15 minutes longer. 6 servings.

All-American Macaroni Casserole (above)

BEEF-CHEESE CASSEROLE

1 1/2 lb. ground beef
1 med. onion, chopped
1 tsp. salt
1/8 tsp. pepper
2 8-oz. cans tomato sauce
1 c. cottage cheese

1 8-oz. package cream cheese
1/4 c. sour cream
1/4 c. chopped green pepper
1/4 c. chopped green onion
1 8-oz. package noodles

Brown the ground beef and onion in a skillet. Add the salt, pepper and tomato sauce and simmer for about 10 minutes. Combine the cottage cheese, cream cheese, sour cream, green pepper and onion. Cook the noodles according to package directions and drain. Place half the noodles in a greased 3-quart casserole and add the cheese mixture. Add remaining noodles and pour beef mixture over noodles. Bake at 350 degrees for 30 minutes. 8-10 servings.

Mrs. Sue T. Glovier, Old Fort, North Carolina

BEEF AND PORK CASSEROLE

1/2 lb. lean ground pork
1/2 lb. ground beef
1 lge. onion, chopped
1 clove of garlic, minced
1 sm. green pepper, chopped

1 No. 2 can tomatoes
Salt and pepper to taste
Chili powder to taste
1 c. grated cheese
1 8-oz. package fine noodles

Brown the meats, onion, garlic and green pepper in a skillet. Add tomatoes and cook until most of the liquid has evaporated. Add the salt, pepper, chili powder and 2/3 of the cheese. Cook the noodles according to package directions and place in a buttered baking dish. Top with the meat mixture and sprinkle with remaining cheese. Chill for 2 hours. Bake, covered, at 300 degrees for 45 minutes. 6 servings.

Mrs. Herman Whitson, Fort Smith, Arkansas

BEEF AND NOODLE CASSEROLE

2 lb. ground beef
1 lge. onion, chopped
Salt to taste
2 pkg. egg noodles
1 can corn
1 can mushroom soup

1 can cream of chicken soup
1 can Mexican corn
1 carton sour cream
Cracker crumbs
Butter

Brown the beef in a skillet with the onion, then add salt. Cook the noodles according to package directions and drain. Mix the noodles, corn, mushroom soup, chicken soup, Mexican corn and sour cream together, then add the beef mixture. Pour into a casserole. Top with cracker crumbs and dot with butter. Bake at 350 degrees for 30 minutes. 10 servings.

Mrs. Ralph V. Earrhardt, Anniston, Alabama

BEEF-NUT CASSEROLE

1 lb. ground beef
1 c. chopped celery
1 1/2 c. chopped onions
1 can cream of mushroom soup
1 can cream of chicken soup

1 soup can milk
1 8-oz. package egg noodles
1 c. chow mein noodles
1/2 c. chopped cashew nuts

Brown the ground beef, celery and onions in a skillet. Add the soups and milk and mix well. Cook the noodles according to package directions. Add to beef mixture and mix well. Place in a large casserole. Bake, covered, at 350 degrees for 1 hour. Remove cover and sprinkle with chow mein noodles and cashew nuts. Bake for 10 minutes longer.

Mrs. F. R. Hamilton, Greensboro, North Carolina

CHEF'S CASSEROLE

1 pkg. egg noodles
1 lb. ground beef
1 sm. onion, chopped
2 tbsp. butter
1 can cream of mushroom soup

1 c. sliced ripe olives
1 tsp. garlic salt
Pepper to taste
1/2 lb. cheese, diced
1/3 c. tomato sauce

Cook the noodles according to package directions and drain. Brown the beef and onion in the butter, then combine all the ingredients and turn into a 2-quart casserole. Bake, covered, at 350 degrees for 1 hour. Serve with grated Parmesan cheese, if desired. 4 servings.

Mrs. Kenneth H. Arnold, Atlanta, Georgia

JIMMY'S FAVORITE CASSEROLE

1 lb. ground round steak
2 tbsp. grated onion
1 tsp. salt
1/2 tsp. pepper
1/4 c. Worcestershire sauce
2 tbsp. butter

2 tbsp. flour
2 c. milk
1 c. grated sharp cheese
1 8-oz. package fine noodles
1 carton sour cream

Cook the ground steak and onion in 2 tablespoons fat in a skillet until brown, then drain. Add the salt, pepper and Worcestershire sauce. Melt the butter in a 1 1/2-quart saucepan. Add flour and cook until smooth. Add the milk and cook, stirring constantly, until smooth. Add the cheese and stir until blended and smooth. Remove from heat and add the beef mixture. Cook the noodles according to package directions and drain. Place alternate layers of noodles, beef sauce and sour cream in a greased 3-quart casserole. Bake at 350 degrees for 20 to 25 minutes. 8 servings.

Mrs. Lillian King Wier, Odem, Texas

LASAGNA LORRAINE

1/2 lb. ground beef	1 tbsp. chopped basil
1 med. onion, chopped fine	Salt and pepper to taste
1 clove of garlic, minced	1 pkg. lasagna
3 tsp. olive oil	1 lb. ricotta cheese
1 16-oz. can tomatoes	1 lb. mozzarella cheese, sliced
1/2 can tomato paste	Grated Parmesan cheese
1 tsp. sugar	

Brown the ground beef, onion and garlic in olive oil in a large frypan. Press the tomatoes through a strainer and add to ground beef mixture. Add the tomato paste, sugar, basil, salt, pepper and 1 cup water and mix well. Simmer for 30 minutes. Cook the lasagna in 4 quarts of rapidly boiling, salted water for 10 to 12 minutes or until tender. Drain, rinse in cold water and drain again. Layer the ground beef sauce, noodles, ricotta cheese, mozzarella cheese and Parmesan cheese in a large casserole until all ingredients are used, ending with Parmesan cheese. Bake at 375 degrees for 30 minutes.

Wanda Thomas, Ocilla, Georgia

TAGLIARINI

1/2 med. green pepper, chopped	1 12-oz. package egg noodles
1 med. onion, chopped	1 No. 303 can cream-style corn
2 cloves of garlic, chopped	Salt and pepper to taste
1 lb. ground beef	1 sm. can sliced mushrooms
1/4 lb. butter	1 sm. can chopped ripe olives
1 qt. tomato juice	Grated sharp cheese
3 c. tomato sauce	

Saute the green pepper, onion, garlic and ground beef in butter in large Dutch oven, then add tomato juice and sauce. Bring to a boil. Add the noodles and cook until tender. Add the corn, seasonings, mushrooms and ripe olives, then pour into a large casserole. Top with cheese. Bake at 350 degrees for 45 minutes. 10 servings.

Mrs. W. F. Delancey, Yazoo City, Mississippi

BAKED-STUFFED RIGATONI

Salt	2 lb. ground beef
3 qt. boiling water	2 eggs, beaten
8 oz. rigatoni	1/2 c. dry bread crumbs
2 tbsp. vegetable shortening	3 tbsp. chopped parsley
3/4 c. chopped onions	Pepper to taste
1 clove of garlic, minced	Tomato Sauce

Add 1 tablespoon salt to boiling water. Add rigatoni so that water continues to boil and cook, stirring occasionally, until tender. Drain in a colander, then rinse with cold water and drain again. Spread rigatoni out on a tray. Melt the shortening in large skillet. Add the onions and garlic and cook over medium heat until golden. Add the beef and cook, stirring constantly, just until lightly browned. Remove from heat and cool slightly. Blend in the eggs, bread crumbs and parsley. Season with salt to taste and pepper. Stuff rigatoni with beef mixture. Arrange the stuffed rigatoni in a shallow 3-quart casserole. Pour the Tomato Sauce over the rigatoni. Bake in 350-degree oven for 30 minutes, spooning sauce over top occasionally. 8-10 servings.

Tomato Sauce

5 slices bacon, diced	3/4 tsp. salt
3/4 c. chopped onions	1/2 tsp. sugar
3/4 c. chopped celery	2 cloves of garlic, crushed
3/4 c. diced carrots	2 28-oz. cans tomatoes in
8 sprigs of parsley	tomato puree
1/2 tsp. thyme leaves	2 10 1/2-oz. cans beef
1 bay leaf	broth

Cook the bacon in a large saucepan or Dutch oven for about 2 minutes. Add the onions, celery and carrots and cook until onions are tender. Stir in remaining ingredients and 2 cups water and simmer for 2 hours, stirring occasionally and adding water, if needed. Press through a sieve or force through a food mill. Add enough water to make 6 cups sauce.

Baked-Stuffed Rigatoni (page 100)

skillet dishes

Take a skillet . . . add your favorite kind of ground beef . . . just the right touch of seasonings . . . a complementary sauce . . . and let the rich aromas emanating from the kitchen attract your hungry family. This is skillet cookery with ground beef — easy, fun, and oh-so-rewarding!

Southern women are famous for their fine skillet cookery. Now they have turned their clever minds toward creating unforgettable ground beef dishes, the best of which are shared with you in the pages which follow.

Excite your family's appetite with Cantonese Style Meatballs. Serve them over noodles or rice, with a green salad and perhaps fruit for dessert. What a flavor treat! For a snappy blend of zesty flavors, feature Pepper Steak with Cheddar Noodles. This dish is certain to become one of your family's all-time favorites, the kind of dish they ask you to serve when they're bringing friends home to dinner.

In fact, this entire section is full of delicious recipes you'll be proud to serve at a quiet family meal or an exciting supper party. Beef Paprikash . . . Salisbury Steaks . . . Curried Beef and Rice . . . marvelous skillet meals prepared with ground beef. Select one of these recipes now, and surprise your family tonight — they'll thank you for it!

ALLEN ORIENTAL

1 lb. hamburger	1 tsp. soy sauce
1 med. onion, sliced	1 bay leaf
1 can beef broth	1 tsp. marjoram
1/2 c. chopped celery	Salt and pepper to taste
1/2 tsp. gumbo file	

Brown hamburger in a skillet over low heat. Add the onion and cook till onion is tender. Add remaining ingredients and heat through. Serve over rice. 2-3 servings.

Mrs. Sharyn Allen, Eglin AFB, Florida

BEEF AND VEGETABLE DISH

2 lb. ground beef	2 c. chopped cabbage
1 1/2 tsp. salt	2 c. diced potatoes
2 c. chopped carrots	1 can English peas

Place the beef in a frying pan and add enough hot water to cover. Add the salt, carrots, cabbage and potatoes. Cover and cook until the vegetables are tender. Remove the cover and add the peas. Simmer, stirring, for 3 to 5 minutes.

Mrs. Mabel Cagle, Collinsville, Alabama

DRUMSTICKS

2 lb. ground beef	2 tsp. salt
1/2 c. finely chopped onion	1 tsp. monosodium glutamate
2 tsp. prepared mustard	Pepper to taste
1 tsp. Worcestershire sauce	1 c. fine dry bread crumbs
2 eggs, beaten	6 tbsp. shortening

Mix the beef with the onion, mustard, Worcestershire sauce and eggs, then add the salt, monosodium glutamate and pepper, mixing well. Divide the mixture into 8 portions. Shape each portion as a drumstick around a skewer, then roll in the bread crumbs. Melt the shortening in a skillet. Place the drumsticks in the skillet and cook over moderate heat, turning carefully to brown all sides. Reduce the heat and continue to cook for 15 minutes, turning occasionally. Serve on a warm platter and garnish with parsley. 8 servings.

Mrs. Mary Dowling, Houston, Texas

GENGHIS KHAN

1 lb. hamburger	1 can Chinese vegetables
1 med. onion, chopped	2 tbsp. cornstarch
1/4 c. butter	1 tbsp. soy sauce
Salt and pepper to taste	1 tsp. sugar
1 c. diced celery	1 can chow mein noodles

Cook the hamburger and onion in butter in a skillet until lightly browned. Add the salt, pepper, celery and 1 1/2 cups water and cover. Simmer for 20 minutes. Drain the Chinese vegetables, then add to hamburger mixture and bring to a boil. Combine the cornstarch, 2 tablespoons cold water, soy sauce and sugar and mix well. Stir into hamburger mixture and cook until slightly thickened, stirring constantly. Serve over the noodles and garnish with green onions and hard-cooked egg slices.

Mrs. J. G. Powers, Monroe, Louisiana

SKILLET LONDON BROIL

2 lb. ground beef	2 tsp. salt
1 tsp. hot sauce	2 tbsp. butter or margarine
1 tbsp. instant minced onion	

Combine ground beef, hot sauce, onion and salt and mix well. Shape into a large patty, about 1 3/4 inches thick. Melt the butter in heavy skillet, then add the patty and cook over medium heat for 10 to 12 minutes on each side.

Hot Buttered Corn

2 1-lb. cans whole kernel	1 tsp. salt
corn	3 tbsp. butter or
1/2 tsp. hot sauce	margarine

Drain the corn, then combine with the hot sauce, salt and butter in a skillet. Cook until heated through, stirring occasionally. Serve with the London Broil. Garnish with green pepper strips and onion rings, if desired. 6-8 servings.

Skillet London Broil (above)

SUKIYAKI-STYLE GROUND BEEF

1 Bermuda onion	1 5-oz. can bamboo shoots
1 tbsp. salad oil	1 tbsp. sugar
1 lb. ground beef	1/3 c. soy sauce
3 stalks celery	1 chicken bouillon cube
6 lge. fresh mushrooms	1/2 lb. spinach
1/4 lb. green beans	

Slice the onion thin and saute in the salad oil in a large frying pan until soft. Add the ground beef and saute for 2 to 3 minutes, stirring with a fork to separate. Cut the celery, mushrooms and beans into thin slices and add with the bamboo shoots, sugar, soy sauce, bouillon cube and 1/2 cup water to the hamburger mixture. Stir to mix, then cover and simmer for 10 minutes. Clean and remove stems from the spinach and arrange on top of the hamburger mixture. Cover and simmer for 5 minutes longer or until the spinach wilts and vegetables are crisp tender. Serve with seasoned rice. 6 servings.

Mrs. J. B. Hand, Bethesda, Maryland

INDIAN BEEF CURRY

1 med. onion, minced	1/8 tsp. ginger
2 tbsp. salad oil	1 1/2 tsp. salt
2 tbsp. ground coriander	1/2 tsp. hot sauce
1/2 tsp. cinnamon	1 lb. ground beef
1/4 tsp. ground cloves	1/2 c. water
1/4 tsp. ground cardamom	1/2 c. evaporated milk
1/2 tsp. chili powder	1 tsp. lemon juice

Cook the onion in the salad oil until golden, then add the spices, salt and hot sauce and mix well. Stir in the ground beef and cook until brown. Add the water and cook until slightly thickened. Blend in the milk and lemon juice, then remove from heat.

Puris

1 c. sifted flour	1/4 tsp. hot sauce
1/2 tsp. salt	1/4 c. water
2 tbsp. butter, melted	Salad oil or shortening

Sift the flour with the salt into a bowl, then add the butter and hot sauce, mixing well with a fork. Stir in the water to make a soft pliable dough. Knead the dough for 5 to 7 minutes or until smooth on a lightly floured surface. Roll dough 1/8 inch thick and cut into 2-inch rounds. Heat about 2 inches of salad oil in a deep fat fryer or heavy skillet to 360 degrees. Fry the rounds, several at a time, for about 1 minute on each side or until golden brown. Drain on paper towels. Garnish beef curry with several rounds and serve remaining rounds separately.

HAMBURGER FRITTERS

1/2 lb. ground beef	1 tsp. lemon juice
3 eggs, separated	1/2 tsp. prepared mustard
1/4 tsp. baking powder	1 tsp. catsup
1/2 tsp. salt	1 tbsp. minced parsley
Dash of pepper	1 tbsp. grated onion

Combine the beef, egg yolks and remaining ingredients except egg whites, then fold in the beaten egg whites. Drop by spoonfuls into large greased skillet. Cook until puffed and brown, then turn and brown remaining side. Serve immediately. 4 servings.

Mrs. Edith Peeks, Lubbock, Texas

HAMBURGER AND PEAS

1 1/2 lb. hamburger	1 can beef broth
1/4 c. chopped onion	1/2 broth can water
1 tsp. monosodium glutamate	1 tbsp. flour
1 tsp. salt	3 tbsp. milk
1 pkg. frozen green peas	

Brown the hamburger and onion in a skillet and drain off excess fat. Add the monosodium glutamate, salt, peas, beef broth and water. Bring to a boil, then reduce heat and simmer for 30 minutes. Combine the flour and milk and add to the meat mixture. Simmer for 5 minutes longer. Serve with noodles or potatoes, if desired. 6 servings.

Mrs. Kay Parker, Cordell, Oklahoma

Indian Beef Curry (page 106)

GROUND ROUND ROULADES

2 lb. ground round	2 dill pickles
2 c. fine soft bread crumbs	1/2 c. finely chopped onion
2 eggs	4 slices bacon, halved
1/2 c. evaporated milk	1 can beef bouillon
1 tsp. salt	1/2 c. water
1/4 tsp. pepper	1/2 c. dry red wine
Prepared mustard	2 tbsp. catsup
1/2 lge. green pepper	

Combine the ground beef, crumbs, eggs, milk, salt and pepper well and divide into 2 parts. Pat each part into a 10-inch square on waxed paper or foil and spread with mustard. Cut each square into quarters. Cut the green pepper into 16 thin strips and quarter the dill pickles lengthwise. Place 1 tablespoon onion, 2 strips of green pepper, 1 slice dill pickle and 1/2 slice bacon near the edge of each ground beef quarter. Roll ground beef mixture around the filling, shaping and patting to form a smooth roll. Brown carefully in small amount of fat over medium heat. Do not turn rolls until crust forms on bottom. Drain off excess fat. Combine remaining ingredients and pour over the rolls. Cover and simmer for 35 to 40 minutes. Transfer roulades to a platter and thicken pan liquid as desired. Pour over roulades to serve. May be made a day in advance and reheated. Roulades freeze well. 8 servings.

Mrs. H. L. Hudgins, Meridian, Mississippi

HAMBURGER SKILLET MEAL

1 lb. hamburger	1 c. drained whole kernel corn
1 c. soft bread crumbs	1 c. sliced onions
1 3/4 tsp. salt	1 c. cooked whole tomatoes
1/8 tsp. pepper	1 c. tomato juice

Combine the hamburger, bread crumbs, 1 teaspoon salt and pepper. Fry in a heavy skillet, stirring frequently, until well browned. Cover with the corn and onions. Sprinkle the remaining salt over the onions and add the tomatoes, but do not stir. Add the tomato juice. Cover and simmer for 20 minutes or until the vegetables are tender. Serve from the skillet over rice. 6 servings.

Mrs. Florence Fisher, Fort Smith, Arkansas

SUMPTUOUS HOMINY BEEF

1 lb. ground beef	1/2 c. water or tomato sauce
2 tbsp. chili seasoning mix	2 c. white hominy
Dash of salt	

Brown the beef in a heavy pot and sprinkle with chili seasoning, mixing well. Add salt, water and hominy. Simmer, covered, until hominy is heated. 4-6 servings.

Mrs. Earl C. Lewis, Chalmette, Louisiana

SAO PAULO BEEF

1 lb. ground beef	1/2 lb. elbow macaroni
1 med. onion, chopped	1 can cream of mushroom soup
1 bell pepper, chopped	

Crumble the ground beef in a skillet and cook until brown. Add the onion and pepper and cook until tender. Cook the macaroni according to package directions and drain. Combine the beef mixture, soup and macaroni and stir over low heat until heated through.

Mrs. Nellie Todd, Yuma, Tennessee

SWEDISH MEATBALLS

1 lb. ground beef	2 tsp. salt
1 lb. ground veal	1 tsp. nutmeg
1 sm. onion, finely chopped	1/8 tsp. ginger
1/2 c. crushed zwieback or	Flour
toasted bread crumbs	2 tbsp. butter
1 egg	1 c. milk

Combine the beef, veal and onion. Add 1/2 cup water to crumbs, then mix and add to meat mixture. Add the egg, 1 1/2 teaspoons salt, 1/2 teaspoon nutmeg and ginger to the meat mixture and mix well. Shape into 40 balls, about the size of a walnut, then dredge in flour. Melt the butter in a large skillet, then add the meatballs and brown on all sides. Cover and cook slowly for 20 minutes. Remove the meatballs from the skillet. Add about 3 tablespoons flour to drippings and stir to loosen particles from pan. Add 1 1/4 cups water, milk, remaining salt and remaining nutmeg. Cook, stirring constantly, until thickened. Arrange meatballs with sauce in serving dish. 8 servings.

Swedish Meatballs (above)

109

VAQUERO BEEF DISH

1 1/2 lb. ground beef	1/2 tsp. oregano
1 c. coarsely chopped onion	1/4 tsp. pepper
1 clove of garlic, minced	1 1-lb. can tomatoes
1 tbsp. shortening	1 6-oz. can tomato paste
2 tsp. salt	2 c. shredded Cheddar cheese
2 tsp. chili powder	1 6-oz. bag corn chips
1 tsp. paprika	

Saute the beef, onion and garlic in the shortening until the onion is soft and the beef is lightly browned. Add the seasonings, tomatoes and tomato paste and stir. Cover and simmer for 25 to 30 minutes or until the beef is cooked and flavors are blended. Stir in 1 cup cheese and allow cheese to melt. Stir in 2 cups corn chips just before serving. Serve over remaining corn chips and sprinkle with remaining cheese. 6 servings.

Mrs. Mart McMillan, Houston, Texas

HAMBURGER POTLUCK

2 tbsp. vegetable oil	1/4 tsp. pepper
1/2 lb. ground beef	1 9-oz. can tomatoes
3/4 c. chopped onion	2 c. cooked seashell macaroni
1 c. sliced celery	1 c. diced American cheese
1 1/2 tsp. salt	

Heat the oil in a skillet, then add the ground beef and cook, stirring frequently, for 5 minutes. Add the onion and celery and cook for 5 minutes longer. Add the salt, pepper and tomatoes and bring to a boil. Stir in the macaroni and cook until liquid is absorbed. Blend in the cheese and heat until cheese is melted.

Mrs. Helen Alders, Douglass, Texas

SKILLET CASSEROLE

1/2 8-oz. package elbow macaroni	1/4 c. diced green pepper
1 tbsp. fat	1 tsp. salt
1/2 lb. ground beef	Dash of pepper
1/4 c. chopped onion	1/2 tsp. Worcestershire sauce
1 3/4 c. canned tomatoes	1 2-oz. can mushrooms
1/2 c. diced celery	4 slices cheese

Cook the macaroni according to package directions, then drain. Heat an electric skillet to 360 degrees and add fat. Add the beef and onion and cook, stirring frequently, until browned. Drain off excess fat. Add the tomatoes, celery, green pepper, seasonings, mushrooms and macaroni and bring to a boil. Cover and simmer at 220 degrees for 30 minutes. Top with cheese slices and cover. Cook for 5 minutes or until cheese is melted. Garnish with parsley and serve hot. 4 servings.

Carla Moss, Wilmington, Delaware

BEEF PORCUPINES

1 lb. ground beef	1 c. rice
3 tbsp. chopped onions	3 tbsp. fat
1 tsp. pepper	2 cans tomato sauce
1 tsp. salt	1 c. water

Combine the ground beef, onions, pepper, salt and rice and form into small balls. Brown lightly in fat in a saucepan and drain off excess fat. Add the tomato sauce and water and cover tightly. Simmer for 45 to 50 minutes or until rice is tender.

Mrs. Floyd V. Lail, Hickory, North Carolina

GOLDEN NUGGET MEATBALLS

1 1/2 lb. ground beef	1 egg, beaten
1 1/2 c. soft bread crumbs	1/3 c. catsup
1/3 c. chopped green pepper	16 3/4-in. cubes sharp
1/4 tsp. dry mustard	Cheddar cheese
1/2 tsp. garlic salt	3 tbsp. lard or drippings
1 tsp. salt	2 8-oz. cans tomato sauce
1/8 tsp. pepper	

Combine the beef, bread crumbs, green pepper, mustard, garlic salt, salt, pepper, egg and catsup and mix well. Shape into 16 balls, allowing 3 to 4 tablespoons per ball. Place a cheese cube in the center of each meatball, shaping the beef mixture around the cheese. Brown the meatballs in the lard, then pour off the drippings. Add the tomato sauce, then cover tightly and simmer for 20 minutes. Remove cover and continue simmering for 5 to 10 minutes or until sauce is slightly thickened. Serve over spaghetti, if desired. 4-6 servings.

Golden Nugget Meatballs (above)

111

BURGUNDY MEATBALLS

1 lb. ground chuck	3/4 c. light cream
1 c. bread crumbs	Flour
1 c. chopped onions	Oil
3/4 tsp. cornstarch	1 c. Burgundy
1/2 tsp. salt	1 1/2 c. water
1/2 tsp. nutmeg	2 beef bouillon cubes
1 egg, well beaten	1 1/2 tsp. sugar

Combine the ground chuck, crumbs, onions, cornstarch, salt, nutmeg, egg and cream and shape into small balls. Roll in flour, then brown in small amount of oil. Combine remaining ingredients in a saucepan and cook over low heat until bouillon cubes are dissolved. Add meatballs and simmer for about 2 hours. 4-6 servings.

Mrs. B. L. Akins, Louisville, Kentucky

HAMBURGER PUFFS

1 lb. ground chuck	1/2 lge. onion, minced
2 tbsp. flour	1 c. evaporated milk
1/2 tsp. Worcestershire sauce	1 egg
1/2 tsp. pepper	Pinch of marjoram
1 tsp. salt	Pinch of thyme (opt.)
2 slices bread, crumbled	Cooking oil

Mix all ingredients except oil and shape into small balls. Place in a bowl and cover. Refrigerate for 2 hours. Brown in small amount of oil in a skillet, turning frequently.

Mrs. E. M. Briggs, Houston, Texas

CANTONESE-STYLE MEATBALLS

1 lb. ground beef	Dash of pepper
1/4 c. fine dry bread crumbs	2/3 c. evaporated milk
2/3 c. chopped onion	2 tbsp. butter
1 tsp. salt	

Combine the ground beef, crumbs, onion, salt, pepper and evaporated milk in a medium mixing bowl and shape into 12 meatballs. Melt the butter in a large skillet over medium heat and brown meatballs in the butter, turning occasionally.

Sauce

1 13 1/2-oz. can pineapple	1/4 c. vinegar
chunks	1/4 c. sugar
1 1/2 tbsp. cornstarch	2 tsp. soy sauce
2 tbsp. water	1 tbsp. butter

1/2 c. sliced green onion
1/2 c. green pepper, cut in
   1/4-in. strips
1 c. sliced celery

1 lge. tomato, cut in wedges
1/4 c. blanched toasted almonds,
   salted

Drain the pineapple and reserve liquid. Mix the cornstarch and water in a bowl until smooth. Add reserved pineapple liquid, vinegar, sugar and soy sauce and pour over meatballs. Bring to a boil and reduce heat. Simmer for 20 minutes. Add butter and stir until melted. Add the pineapple, onion, green pepper, celery and tomato and stir lightly. Cover and cook over low heat for 10 minutes longer. Sprinkle with almonds and serve over rice, if desired. 6 servings.

Mrs. Perry Schaeffer, Nashville, Tennessee

MEATBALLS IN ONION GRAVY

1 lb. ground beef
2 slices bread, crumbled
1 egg
1/2 c. milk
1 tsp. salt
1/8 tsp. pepper

1/2 tsp. tarragon
Flour
2 tbsp. shortening
1 env. onion soup mix
1/2 c. grated cheese

Blend the beef, bread, egg, milk, salt, pepper and tarragon in a bowl, then shape into 18 meatballs. Roll in flour and brown in shortening in a skillet over moderate heat. Dissolve the soup mix in 2 cups hot water and add to meatballs. Cover. Cook over low heat for 20 to 25 minutes or until meatballs are done. Mix 2 tablespoons flour and 1/4 cup water until smooth and stir into meatball mixture. Cook until smooth and thickened. Sprinkle with cheese just before serving.

Mrs. Thomas Cameron, Hondo, Texas

KOTTBULLAR

1 lb. ground beef
1/4 c. fine dry bread crumbs
2/3 c. chopped onions
1 tsp. salt
Dash of pepper
1 2/3 c. evaporated milk
4 tbsp. butter

2 beef bouillon cubes
1 1/2 c. boiling water
1/3 c. flour
1/2 tsp. allspice
1 tbsp. lemon juice
1 8-oz. package noodles
1 tsp. poppy seed

Combine the ground beef, bread crumbs, onions, salt, pepper and 2/3 cup evaporated milk and shape into balls. Brown in 2 tablespoons butter in a skillet. Dissolve the bouillon cubes in 1 cup boiling water and pour over meatballs. Bring to a boil over medium heat and cover. Simmer for 15 minutes. Remove from heat and sprinkle with flour and allspice. Stir in remaining evaporated milk and boiling water and cook, uncovered, over low heat, stirring occasionally, until sauce is thickened. Stir in the lemon juice. Cook the noodles according to package directions and drain. Toss with remaining butter and poppy seed and serve with meatballs.

Betty Mixon, Jackson, Mississippi

SKIL-A-RONI MEATBALLS

1 lb. ground beef
1 onion, minced
1/2 green pepper, minced
1/2 c. instant nonfat dry milk
Salt and pepper to taste
2 tbsp. salad oil

1 lge. can macaroni in cheese
   sauce
1 sm. can sliced mushrooms
1/4 c. chili sauce or catsup
1 tsp. prepared mustard

Mix the beef, onion, green pepper, milk and seasonings thoroughly and shape into 12 balls. Brown in hot oil in a large skillet and drain off fat. Combine remaining ingredients and mix with meatballs. Cover and cook over low heat for about 10 minutes. 4 servings.

Mrs. Landwell McCall, Lenoir, North Carolina

MEAT PANCAKES

3 eggs, separated
1/2 lb. ground beef
1/4 tsp. baking powder
1/2 tsp. salt

Dash of pepper
1 tsp. lemon juice
1 tbsp. minced parsley
1 tbsp. grated onion

Beat the egg yolks lightly in a bowl. Add remaining ingredients except egg whites and mix well. Fold in stiffly beaten egg whites. Drop by spoonfuls onto greased, hot griddle and cook until puffed and brown. Turn and brown other side. Serve at once with mushroom sauce or creamed vegetable, if desired. 6 servings.

Betty Sue Brown, Kosciusko, Mississippi

MEXICAN EGGPLANT SKILLET

1 lb. lean ground beef
1/4 c. chopped onion
1 tbsp. flour
1 8-oz. can seasoned tomato
   sauce
1/4 c. chopped green pepper
1 tsp. oregano

1/2 to 1 teaspoon chili powder
Salt
1 sm. eggplant, cut in 1/2-in.
   slices
Pepper to taste
1 c. shredded American process
   cheese

Cook the beef and onion in small amount of hot fat in a skillet until beef is brown. Spoon off excess fat. Sprinkle flour over beef mixture and stir. Add the tomato sauce, green pepper, oregano, chili powder and 1/2 teaspoon salt and mix well. Season eggplant with salt to taste and pepper and arrange over beef mixture. Cover and simmer for 10 to 15 minutes or until eggplant is tender. Top with cheese. 4 servings.

Mrs. Madge G. Young, Annapolis, Maryland

CLUB NIGHT SPECIAL

1 1/2 lb. ground chuck
1 sm. onion, diced

1 1/2 c. water
2 sm. cans tomato sauce

1 can lima beans
1 can Mexican-style corn

2 c. noodles, cooked
Salt and pepper to taste

Brown the ground chuck and onion in a skillet and drain off excess fat. Add remaining ingredients and simmer for 20 minutes. 8 servings.

Mrs. J. T. Moon, New Orleans, Louisiana

NOODLE SKILLET SCRAMBLE

1   8-oz. can tomato sauce
    with tomato bits
1/2 c. beef bouillon or broth
2 tsp. salt
1/4 tsp. coarsely ground
    pepper
1 1/2 tsp. oregano leaves
1/4 tsp. thyme leaves, crushed
1 tsp. Worcestershire sauce

3 tbsp. salad oil
1 lb. ground beef chuck
1 1/4 c. chopped onions
1 clove of garlic, crushed
1 med. green pepper, diced
2 c. sliced celery
1/2 c. chopped parsley
8 oz. wide egg noodles

Combine the tomato sauce, bouillon, salt, pepper, oregano, thyme and Worcestershire sauce in a bowl, then set aside. Heat the oil in large skillet over medium heat, then add the beef and cook, stirring constantly, until browned. Remove the beef with slotted spoon and add to the tomato mixture. Saute the onions, garlic, green pepper and celery in drippings in skillet until crisp-tender. Cover skillet and cook for about 6 to 8 minutes longer over low heat, stirring occasionally. Stir in the parsley. Cook the noodles according to package directions and drain in a colander. Remove the vegetables from the skillet. Place the noodles in the skillet, then place the beef mixture in the center. Arrange the vegetables around the edge and heat through. May combine all ingredients in the skillet and toss lightly, if desired.

Noodle Skillet Scramble (above)

BEEF ANDALOUSE

2 tbsp. shortening	1/8 tsp. pepper
1 lb. ground beef	2 tsp. Worcestershire sauce
1 c. chopped onions	3 c. tomato juice
2 tsp. salt	1 5-oz. package noodles
1 tsp. celery salt	1 c. sour cream

Melt the shortening in a skillet. Add the ground beef and onions and cook until brown. Add seasonings, tomato juice and noodles and bring to a boil. Reduce heat and simmer for 30 minutes. Add sour cream and heat through. 6 servings.

Mrs. Jean T. Sutherland, Brownwood, Texas

BEEF PAPRIKASH

1/4 c. oil	1 6-oz. can mushrooms
1 1/2 lb. ground beef	1 can cream of chicken soup
1 c. chopped onions	1 c. sour cream
2 tbsp. flour	1 12-oz. package noodles,
2 tsp. salt	cooked
1 tsp. paprika	1/2 c. chopped green pepper
1/4 tsp. pepper	1/4 c. chopped parsley

Heat the oil in a large skillet. Add the ground beef and onions and brown lightly. Stir in the flour and seasonings. Add the mushrooms and soup and cook over low heat for about 10 minutes. Blend in the sour cream and remove from heat. Combine the noodles with green pepper and parsley. Serve ground beef mixture over noodle mixture. 6-8 servings.

Mrs. R. B. Williams, Little Rock, Arkansas

FILLED NOODLES

2 eggs, beaten	1 sm. onion, chopped fine
1/2 tsp. baking powder	2 tbsp. cooking oil
Flour	1 tbsp. butter
3/4 lb. ground beef	1/2 tsp. chili powder
Salt	1 No. 2 can tomatoes
Pepper to taste	

Combine the eggs, 2 tablespoons water and baking powder and add enough flour to make a stiff dough. Roll out thin on a floured surface and cut in 4-inch squares. Cook the beef, salt to taste, pepper and onion in oil in a skillet until brown. Place small amount of beef filling on each square. Fold over and seal edges. Combine 4 cups water, butter, 1/2 teaspoon salt, chili powder and tomatoes in a saucepan and cook until flavors are blended, breaking up tomatoes. Add noodles to tomato sauce and cook for 20 minutes.

Mrs. Willie Grinke, Fredericksburg, Texas

HAMBURGER DINNER

1 lb. hamburger	Salt and pepper to taste
2 med. onions, chopped	1 pkg. noodles, cooked
1 lge. can tomato sauce	

Crumble the hamburger and cook with onions in small amount of fat in a skillet until brown. Add the tomato sauce, salt and pepper and simmer for 10 minutes. Place the noodles on a platter and spoon beef mixture over noodles.

Mrs. Laura Hamilton, Dothan, Alabama

SUPREME HAMBURGER NOODLES

1 c. chopped onions	1 tsp. salt
1/2 c. chopped green pepper	1 1/2 tsp. celery salt
2 tbsp. fat	Pepper to taste
1 lb. ground beef	2 tsp. Worcestershire sauce
3 c. small noodles	1 c. sour cream
3 c. cocktail vegetable juice	1 3-oz. can mushrooms

Cook the onions and green pepper in fat in a skillet until tender. Add the beef and brown lightly. Stir in the noodles. Combine the vegetable juice, salt, celery salt, pepper and Worcestershire sauce and pour over noodle mixture. Bring to a boil and cover. Reduce heat and simmer for 10 minutes or until noodles are tender. Stir in the sour cream and mushrooms and heat through. 6 servings.

Mrs. Carl Smith, Port Arthur, Texas

PEPPER STEAK WITH CHEDDAR NOODLES

1/4 c. butter	1 tbsp. cornstarch
1 1/2 lb. ground beef	2 tbsp. water
1/8 tsp. garlic powder	2 tbsp. soy sauce
1/3 c. chopped onions	1 tsp. sugar
1 1/2 green peppers, cut in strips	1/2 tsp. salt
1 1-lb. can tomatoes	3 c. wide noodles
1 beef bouillon cube	1 c. shredded Cheddar cheese

Melt the butter in a 10-inch skillet. Add the beef and garlic powder and cook, stirring occasionally, until browned. Remove beef from skillet. Add onions and green peppers to the skillet and saute for 2 minutes. Return beef to skillet with tomatoes and bouillon cube. Blend the cornstarch, water, soy sauce, sugar and salt and add to beef mixture. Cook, stirring, for 2 minutes. Cook the noodles according to package directions and drain. Toss with cheese. Serve beef mixture over noodle mixture. 8 servings.

Mrs. Rena D. Marstiller, Valley Mills, Texas

Speedy Stroganoff (below)

SPEEDY STROGANOFF

1 lb. ground beef	1 2-oz. can sliced mushrooms,
1/2 c. chopped onion	drained
1/2 c. chopped celery	1 tsp. garlic salt
1 can cream of celery soup	1 c. sour cream

Brown the beef, onion and celery in a skillet, then add the soup, mushrooms and garlic salt. Cook for 5 minutes. Add the sour cream and heat, over low heat, to serving temperature. Serve over noodles or rice.

BARBECUED HAMBURGERS

1/2 c. soft bread crumbs	1 tbsp. vinegar
1/4 c. water	2 tbsp. Worcestershire sauce
1/2 lb. ground round steak	1 tbsp. sugar
Salt and pepper to taste	1 onion, chopped fine
2 tbsp. fat	1 sm. clove of garlic, chopped
1 c. catsup	fine

Moisten the crumbs with water, then press out moisture. Add the ground steak, salt and pepper and blend thoroughly. Shape into 4 patties. Brown lightly in fat in a skillet. Stir in remaining ingredients and simmer, covered, for about 30 minutes or until patties are done, adding water, if necessary. Serve on toasted buns or over hot rice.

Mrs. Charles Snook, III, Spartanburg, South Carolina

BEEF PATTIES

1 lb. ground beef	1 egg
1/2 sm. can evaporated milk	1/2 c. rolled oats

1/4 c. cracker crumbs
Dash of pepper
Salt to taste

1/4 c. thick chili sauce
1/4 c. butter
1 1/2 tsp. Worcestershire sauce

Place all ingredients except butter and Worcestershire sauce in a large mixing bowl and mix thoroughly. Shape into patties. Melt the butter in a skillet and add Worcestershire sauce. Add the patties and cook for 5 to 10 minutes on each side. 4-6 servings.

Flora Warf, Nunnelly, Tennessee

PEPPERED HAMBURGERS

1 1/4 lb. ground beef
1 1/2 tsp. salt
1 tsp. paprika
1/2 tsp. pepper
1 egg yolk
6 tbsp. cola beverage

3/4 tbsp. flour
1 onion, sliced
1 green pepper, cut in rings
1 red pepper, cut in rings
Butter or margarine

Combine the ground beef, salt, paprika, pepper, egg yolk, cola beverage and flour and mix well. Chill for about 1 hour. Saute the onion and the green and red peppers in a small amount of butter in a skillet until soft, then remove and set aside. Shape the beef mixture into thick patties and cook in the skillet until done and browned. Top with the onion mixture and serve.

Photograph for this recipe on page 102.

BEEF PATTIES IN SOUP

1 1/2 lb. ground beef
1 egg
1 c. rolled oats
1 tsp. salt

3 tbsp. onion soup mix
1 can cream of chicken soup
1 soup can milk

Mix the ground beef, egg, oats, salt and onion soup mix and shape into patties. Brown on both sides in a skillet. Blend the soup and milk and pour over beef patties. Simmer, covered, for 20 minutes.

Mrs. John Monroe, Jonesboro, Arkansas

BREAKFAST HAMBURGERS

1/2 c. milk
1 slice bread
1 lb. hamburger
1 egg
1 tsp. salt

1/2 tsp. pepper
Garlic salt to taste
Sage to taste
Flour

Pour the milk over bread in a bowl and let soften. Add the hamburger, egg and seasonings and shape into patties. Dredge with flour. Fry in small amount of fat in a skillet until brown. Serve with eggs.

Mrs. Ray Welch, Junction, Texas

Surprise Beef Patties (below)

SURPRISE BEEF PATTIES

2 slices bacon	1/4 tsp. garlic salt
1 lb. ground beef	Dash of pepper
1 c. cooked chopped spinach,	1/4 c. chopped onion
drained	1 can tomato soup
1/2 c. fine dry bread crumbs	1/2 c. water

Cook the bacon in a skillet until crisp, then remove and crumble. Combine the beef, spinach, crumbs, garlic salt and pepper and shape into 4 oval patties. Saute the onion in the drippings in the skillet, then remove with a slotted spoon and set aside. Brown the patties in the drippings, then pour off the fat. Add the soup, water, onion and bacon and cover. Cook over low heat for 20 minutes, stirring occasionally. 4 servings.

HAMBURGER STEAKS IN SPANISH SAUCE

1 1/2 lb. ground beef	1 tbsp. finely chopped mango
1 egg	pepper (opt.)
1 c. cracker crumbs	2 tsp. salt
1 med. onion, finely chopped	1/2 tsp. pepper
1/2 c. evaporated milk	

Combine all ingredients and shape into 6 patties. Cook in lightly greased electric skillet at 375 degrees until steaks are brown on both sides.

Sauce

1 tbsp. Worcestershire sauce	1 tbsp. sugar
1 8-oz. can tomato sauce	1 tbsp. chili powder
1/2 c. water	1/2 tsp. salt

Combine all ingredients and pour over steaks. Reduce heat to 250 degrees and simmer until sauce is thickened and steaks are tender. 6 servings.

Louise Johnson, Rockville, Indiana

COUNTRY-FRIED CHUCK

1 1/2 lb. ground chuck	1 c. flour
3 tsp. salt	3 tbsp. fat
1/2 tsp. pepper	2 1/2 c. milk

Combine the ground chuck, 2 teaspoons salt, pepper and 3/4 cup flour and mix well. Roll out on a board about 1/2 inch thick and cut into 4-inch square pieces. Place in hot fat in a skillet and cook until lightly browned. Remove from skillet and place on a platter. Add remaining flour to skillet and cook until browned, stirring constantly. Add the milk and remaining salt and cook until thick, stirring frequently. Pour over steaks. 5 servings.

Mrs. Paul Smeltzer, Church Hill, Tennessee

CUTLETS IN MUSHROOM SAUCE

2 lb. lean ground beef	1/4 tsp. pepper
1 c. milk	1/4 c. flour
1 tbsp. Worcestershire sauce	1/4 c. cooking oil
Dash of garlic salt	1 can cream of mushroom soup
1 tsp. salt	

Mix the beef, 1/2 cup milk and seasonings in a bowl. Shape into thin, oblong patties and dip into flour. Brown in oil in a skillet. Drain off fat. Dilute soup with remaining milk and pour over patties. Cover and simmer for 10 minutes. 10 servings.

Ruby Robertson Duncan, Sanderson, Texas

SKILLET MEAL

1 lb. ground beef	2 tbsp. shortening
1/4 c. wheat germ	1/2 c. water
Salt and pepper	4 med. potatoes, grated
1 clove of garlic, minced	4 med. carrots, sliced thin
1/2 c. milk	1 green pepper, quartered
1 egg	

Combine the ground beef, wheat germ, 1 teaspoon salt, 1/4 teaspoon pepper, garlic, milk and egg and mix well. Shape into 4 patties. Brown on both sides in shortening in a large skillet. Pour off grease and add the water. Sprinkle potatoes over patties and place carrots and green pepper over potatoes. Season to taste and cover. Simmer for 20 minutes or until vegetables are done. 4 servings.

Mrs. Frank Smith, Birmingham, Alabama

SALISBURY STEAKS

2 strips bacon, diced	1/2 tsp. salt
1 lb. hamburger	Pepper to taste
2 tsp. chopped onion	Cooking oil

Mix all ingredients except oil and shape into 6 oval patties. Brown in small amount of oil in a skillet, then remove from skillet. Pour off all except 2 tablespoons oil from the skillet.

Sauce

1 tbsp. chopped onion	1 bay leaf
1/2 tbsp. minced green pepper	1 tsp. sugar
2 tbsp. flour	Salt and pepper to taste
1/2 can tomatoes	1/2 c. water
1/2 tsp. celery salt	

Add the onion and green pepper to oil in the skillet and cook until tender. Stir in the flour. Add remaining ingredients and mix well. Add patties and simmer for 45 minutes.

Mrs. H. L. Shearer, Atlanta, Georgia

SKILLET PIZZABURGER

1 1/2 lb. ground beef	6 slices mozzarella cheese
1/4 c. finely chopped green	1 can tomato soup
pepper	2 tbsp. water
1 tsp. salt	2 tbsp. dry red wine
1/8 tsp. pepper	Dash of crushed oregano

Mix the ground beef, green pepper, salt and pepper and shape into 12 patties. Place 1 slice cheese on 6 patties and cover with remaining patties. Press edges together. Brown patties in large skillet and pour off all except 1 tablespoon drippings. Stir in the soup, water, wine and oregano and cover. Cook over low heat for 15 minutes, stirring occasionally.

Elizabeth Stacey, Vicksburg, Mississippi

CURRIED BEEF AND RICE

1 lb. ground beef	1 c. chopped potatoes
1 lge. onion, chopped	1 pkg. frozen peas
2 tbsp. cooking oil	1/4 tsp. garlic powder
1 c. rice	1/2 tsp. curry powder
1 can tomato soup	1/2 tsp. salt
2 1/2 soup cans water	Sour cream or yogurt

Saute the beef and onion in oil in a large frypan until onion is lightly browned. Add the rice, soup and water, stirring well. Add the potatoes, peas, garlic powder, curry powder and salt. Cover and bring to a boil. Reduce heat and simmer for 15 minutes. Top with sour cream and serve. 4 servings.

Niva J. Reddick, Largo, Florida

BEEF-BEAN-RICE SKILLET MEAL

1 lb. ground beef	1 tsp. salt
1 med. onion, chopped	1 can tomatoes
2 tbsp. cooking oil	1 can kidney beans
1 tbsp. pepper	1 c. instant rice
2 tbsp. chili powder	

Brown the beef and onion in oil in an electric skillet, then add the remaining ingredients. Cook on high temperature for 5 minutes. Cover and turn off heat, then let stand for 25 minutes before serving. 6 servings.

Mrs. John Newkirk, Hot Springs, Arkansas

BUTTERMILK STROGANOFF

1/2 c. chopped onion	1 tbsp. cornstarch
1/4 c. butter or margarine	1 sm. can water chestnuts
1 lb. ground beef	1 sm. can mushroom pieces
1 tsp. salt	1 can cream of chicken soup
1 tsp. pepper	1 c. buttermilk
1/4 tsp. paprika	3/4 c. rice, cooked
1/4 tsp. monosodium glutamate	1 can chow mein noodles

Brown the onion in the butter, then add the ground beef, salt, pepper, paprika and monosodium glutamate. Cook until beef loses red color. Add the cornstarch and stir well. Drain the water chestnuts and then slice. Add to the beef mixture with the mushrooms and soup. Cook over low heat for 10 minutes. Remove from heat, then add the buttermilk and heat, stirring, until bubbly. Serve over rice and top with chow mein noodles. 6 servings.

Mrs. Joe Alexander, Livingston, Alabama

FRIED BEEF WITH RICE

1 c. cooked rice	1/4 c. soy sauce
1/4 lb. ground beef	2 slightly beaten eggs
1 sm. onion, diced	

Chill the rice overnight. Fry the ground beef and onion in a skillet until lightly browned, then add the rice and fry for 10 minutes, stirring occasionally. Add the soy sauce and 1/4 cup water. Pour the eggs over the rice mixture and cover. Cook over low heat for 10 minutes. May substitute bacon, shrimp or flaked crab for ground beef.

Mrs. Karen Wright, Altus, Oklahoma

Mexihash (below)

MEXIHASH

4 slices bacon	1 15-oz. can Spanish rice
1/2 lb. ground beef	1/4 c. water
1/2 c. chopped onion	1 tsp. salt

Fry the bacon in a skillet over medium heat until crisp. Remove the bacon, then drain and crumble. Pour off all but 2 tablespoons dripping, then add the ground beef and onion and brown. Stir in the rice, water, salt and crumbled bacon and cook until heated through. 4 servings.

GROUND BEEF CURRY

1/2 c. chopped onions	1/4 tsp. curry powder
1 lb. ground beef	Dash of garlic salt
1 can mushroom soup	3/4 c. grated cheese
1/2 c. milk	1 c. thinly sliced celery
1/2 tsp. salt	1 c. cooked rice

Saute the onions and ground beef in a skillet until onions are soft. Combine the soup, milk, seasonings, cheese, celery and rice and mix well. Pour into the skillet and simmer for 15 minutes. Serve over rice or noodles. 4 servings.

Mrs. Sharon Gillis, Wilson, North Carolina

LEBANESE CABBAGE ROLLS

1/2 c. rice, washed	3 to 4 tbsp. cooking oil
1 lb. ground beef	2 to 3 lb. cabbage
Salt and pepper to taste	1 No. 2 can tomatoes
Dash of cinnamon	1 No. 2 can water

Combine the rice with the beef, salt, pepper, cinnamon and oil and mix thoroughly. Cover and set aside. Remove the core from the cabbage and place in pan of boiling water, whole side down, and cook until the leaves separate easily. Remove cabbage from water and remove the leaves, one at a time. Trim off stiff part of leaves. Fill the leaves with the beef mixture and roll up. Stack the cabbage rolls in a large Dutch oven, lining up 1 layer on the bottom, then placing the next layer crosswise. Continue until all cabbage rolls are in the Dutch oven. Mash the tomatoes in the juice and combine with the water. Season with salt, then pour over the cabbage rolls. Simmer for at least 45 minutes.

Mrs. Ben Catalina, Clarksdale, Mississippi

HAMBURGER AND RICE IN A SKILLET

1 lb. hamburger	1 c. rice
1/2 c. diced celery	1 can bouillon

Brown the hamburger and celery in an electric skillet, then add the rice, bouillon and 1 can water. Cover and cook for about 30 to 45 minutes or until rice is tender. 4 servings.

Mrs. Patsy Stephens, Senatobia, Mississippi

ARROZ CON CARNE

2 tbsp. shortening	1/8 tsp. pepper
1 lb. coarsely ground beef	1/4 tsp. thyme
1/2 c. chopped onion	1 can tomato soup
1/3 c. chopped green pepper	1 soup can water
1 clove of garlic, minced	2/3 c. rice
1 tsp. salt	

Melt the shortening in an electric skillet, then add the ground beef and brown. Add the remaining ingredients except the rice, stirring well. Sprinkle the rice over the top and cover. Turn the control to lowest temperature when steam appears and cook for 35 minutes. Do not remove cover but stir well before serving. 4-6 servings.

Willie Hawkins, Lovelady, Texas

ONE-DISH MEAL

1 lb. ground beef	1/4 tsp. garlic powder
1/4 c. chopped onions	1 can red kidney beans
4 tbsp. shortening	1 tbsp. pepper
1 c. rice	1 can tomatoes
2 tsp. salt	

Saute the beef and onions in the shortening, then add the rice and brown. Add the remaining ingredients and bring to a boil. Cover and reduce heat, then simmer for 30 minutes, adding water if needed.

Mrs. C. W. McDaniel, Summit, Mississippi

RUSSIAN RECHAUFFE

1 4-oz. can sliced mushrooms	1/4 tsp. pepper
2 lb. ground beef round	1 tbsp. Worcestershire sauce
1 lge. onion, chopped	1 tbsp. cornstarch
1 clove of garlic, minced	1/2 c. cooking sherry
2 tbsp. bacon drippings	1 c. sour cream
1 sm. can tomato sauce	5 c. cooked rice
1 tsp. salt	

Drain the mushrooms, reserving the liquid. Brown the beef, onion and garlic in bacon drippings, then add the mushrooms, tomato sauce, salt, pepper and Worcestershire sauce. Simmer for 1 hour. Mix the cornstarch with the reserved mushroom liquid and stir into the skillet. Simmer for 30 minutes longer, then add the sherry and sour cream and serve over rice. 6-8 servings.

Mrs. Shirley Carter, Atlanta, Georgia

SPANISH RICE

1 lb. ground beef chuck	1 5-oz. can tomato sauce
2 tbsp. bacon drippings	Salt to taste
1 med. onion, chopped	1/2 c. water
3 tbsp. diced green pepper	2 c. instant rice
1 3 1/2-oz. can mushrooms	

Brown the ground beef in the bacon drippings, then add the onion, green pepper, mushrooms, tomato sauce, salt and water. Simmer for at least 2 hours or longer, adding water if needed. Add the rice and cover. Cook for 15 minutes longer. 4-6 servings.

Mrs. J. E. Balkcom, Jacksonville, Florida

TEXAS HASH

1 lge. onion, sliced	1 No. 2 can tomatoes
1 lge. green pepper, chopped	1 1/2 tsp. salt
1 lb. ground beef	1 1/2 tsp. chili powder
1 c. instant rice	

Cook the onion and green pepper in 3 tablespoons fat in electric skillet until onions are golden and peppers are tender. Add the ground beef and cook until browned. Add the rice, tomatoes, salt and chili powder and cover. Cook at 325 degrees until liquid is absorbed and rice is tender. 6 servings.

Mrs. Gladys Mathews, Wilmington, Delaware

OLIVE CAPER

1 onion, chopped	1 can tomato sauce
1 bell pepper, chopped	1 tsp. capers
1 clove of garlic, minced	1/2 c. raisins
1 lb. ground beef	1 sm. bottle stuffed olives

Cook the onion, bell pepper and garlic in small amount of fat in a skillet over low heat until tender. Add the ground beef and brown. Add the tomato sauce, capers and raisins and simmer for 10 minutes. Drain the olives and add to beef mixture. Heat through. Serve on rice, if desired.

Mrs. B. Thomas Recio, Huntsville, Alabama

SKILLET BEEF LOAF DINNER

1 egg, lightly beaten	2 tbsp. cooking oil
3/4 c. fine soft bread crumbs	2 c. thinly sliced onions
1/2 c. catsup	3 c. sliced potatoes
2 tbsp. minced onion	1 1/2 c. sliced carrots
1 tbsp. salt	1 c. sliced celery
1 tsp. Worcestershire sauce	1 1/2 c. sliced zucchini
1 lb. ground beef chuck	

Combine the egg, crumbs, catsup, minced onion, 1 teaspoon salt and Worcestershire sauce, then add the beef and mix thoroughly with a fork. Shape into a thick 6-inch patty. Place the beef patty in the center of a large skillet with oil, then sprinkle the sliced onions around the patty. Brown the patty on both sides, turning carefully with pancake turner and spatula. Stir the onions frequently as the patty browns. Arrange separate groups of potatoes, carrots, celery and zucchini in large second skillet. Add 1/2 cup water and sprinkle with remaining salt. Cover and parboil for 5 minutes. Push the onions together to one side of skillet. Remove the parboiled vegetables from the skillet with a slotted spoon and arrange around the patty. Bake at 350 degrees for about 40 minutes or until beef is cooked and vegetables are tender. Turn vegetables over gently to coat with the pan juice. 4 servings.

Skillet Beef Loaf Dinner (above)

TAMALE SKILLET

1 lb. ground beef	2 tsp. chili powder
1 sm. onion, minced	2 tsp. garlic powder
1 sm. green pepper, diced	1 tsp. parsley flakes
2 8-oz. cans tomato sauce	1 tsp. Worcestershire sauce
1 8-oz. can whole kernel corn	Salt and pepper to taste
10 to 12 black olives, chopped	

Brown the beef, onion and green pepper in 3 tablespoons fat, stirring with fork to separate beef. Add the tomato sauce, corn, olives and seasonings, then simmer for 30 to 45 minutes, until mixture is heated through and flavors are blended. Serve hot with rice, noodles or mashed potatoes. 4-6 servings.

Mrs. Eva Kelly, Roanoke, Virginia

SOUTH AMERICAN LENTILS

1 lb. dry lentils	3 lb. ground beef
1/2 lb. bacon, diced	Salt to taste
1 lge. onion, chopped	

Soak the lentils in water to cover for several hours or overnight. Saute the bacon slightly, then add the onion, beef, lentils and enough water to barely cover mixture. Simmer, uncovered, until lentils are tender and mixture is mushy. Add salt and serve hot. 12 servings.

Mrs. Aleta Gomez, Tampa, Florida

SOPA DE FIDEO

2 tbsp. shortening	1 1/2 c. yellow whole kernel
1/2 lb. vermicelli, broken	corn
1 lb. ground beef	1 to 3 tsp. chili powder
3 cloves of garlic, minced	1 tsp. salt
2 c. thinly sliced onions	1 tsp. pepper
1/2 c. finely chopped green	1 No. 2 1/2 can tomatoes
pepper	8 oz. sliced American cheese
2 c. thinly sliced celery	

Preheat an electric skillet to 300 degrees. Melt the shortening, then add the vermicelli and saute until lightly browned, stirring occasionally. Add the beef and cook, stirring occasionally until beef loses red color. Stir in the remaining ingredients except cheese and add 1 cup water. Reduce temperature to 200 degrees. Simmer, covered, for 25 minutes. Place the cheese slices over top and cover. Cook for 5 minutes longer or until cheese is melted. 8-10 servings.

Mrs. Inez Culp, Memphis, Tennessee

SPAGHETTI ITALIANO

2 lb. ground beef	2 cans tomatoes
1 med. onion, chopped	1 lge. can tomato sauce
2 cloves of garlic, chopped	Salt to taste
1 c. chopped celery	Cayenne pepper to taste
2 green peppers, chopped	1 pkg. spaghetti

Brown the ground beef, onion, garlic, celery and green peppers in a skillet. Bring the tomatoes to a boil in a Dutch oven, then add the beef mixture and mix well. Stir in the tomato sauce, salt and cayenne pepper and cook over medium heat for about 1 hour and 30 minutes. Cook the spaghetti according to package directions and drain, then stir into the sauce.

Mrs. Howard Sitz, Gadsden, Alabama

SWEET-SOUR RED BEANS WITH BEEF

1/4 lb. ground beef	1 tbsp. parsley
1/4 c. vegetable oil	1/2 tsp. salt
1 med. onion, chopped	1/4 tsp. pepper
1 green pepper, chopped	1/2 tsp. oregano
2 c. canned tomatoes	2 c. red kidney beans
1 tbsp. chili sauce	1 12-oz. can whole kernel
1 tbsp. sweet pickle relish	corn
1 tbsp. brown sugar	Juice of 1 lemon

Brown the beef in oil, then add the onion and cook slowly for 5 minutes. Add the green pepper, tomatoes and seasonings and simmer for 10 minutes. Drain the beans and corn, then add to beef mixture and heat thoroughly, but do not boil. Stir in the lemon juice. 4 servings.

Myrtice Dobson, Resaca, Georgia

TEEN-AGERS DELIGHT

1 med. onion, chopped	1 tbsp. catsup
2 tbsp. shortening	1 tsp. mustard
1 lb. hamburger	1 1/2 c. chopped celery (opt.)
1 tsp. salt	1 can cream of tomato soup
1/2 tsp. pepper	1 tsp. chili powder
1 tsp. Worcestershire sauce	1 tsp. Italian seasoning

Saute the onion in shortening until golden brown, then add the hamburger, salt and pepper and cook until the hamburger is browned. Add the remaining ingredients, then cover and simmer for 30 minutes. Serve on rice or toasted buns.

Nedra Smith, Nanafalia, Alabama

pies

Pies with ground beef — what marvelous family or company's-coming fare! Meat pies have a long tradition in southern cuisine — and generations of imaginative southern women have created memorable recipes for them. Some of the most richly flavored and family-pleasing pies are those prepared with ground beef. And in the pages of this section, you'll discover many ground beef pie recipes certain to be big hits with your hungry family — as they have been with families throughout the Southland.

For the cheese lover, there's a Cheeseburger Pie, hot and dripping with delicious — and nutritious — melted cheese. If your family enjoys a south-of-the-border flavor, introduce them to Chili Con Carne Pie — a beef-and-cornbread blend that's the southern version of a dish that originated in Mexico. And don't forget that all-American favorite, pizza pie. Let your family prepare individual pizzas: have various toppings available and let each person create his own version of this flavorful dish. What fun! And one of the best of the old-time meat pies is Shepherd's Pie, a delightful blend of meat, vegetables, and rich gravy.

On a cold and rainy night, warm your family by serving one of these meat-packed pies. They'll welcome ground beef in this new guise — and you'll welcome their heartfelt compliments!

131

Ripe Olive Bridies (below)

RIPE OLIVE BRIDIES

1 lb. ground lean beef	1/3 c. beef broth
1 tbsp. bacon drippings	1 c. canned pitted California
1 med. onion, chopped	ripe olives
1/4 tsp. powdered thyme	1/4 c. finely chopped
1 1/4 tsp. salt	parsley
1/8 tsp. pepper	2 sticks pastry mix
1 tsp. Worcestershire sauce	1 egg
1 tbsp. flour	

Cook the beef in bacon drippings until lightly browned, then add the onion and cover. Cook until the onion is soft. Mix in the thyme, salt, pepper, Worcestershire sauce and flour, then stir in the broth. Cook for about 10 minutes, stirring occasionally, until slightly thickened. Stir in the ripe olives and parsley and cool slightly. Prepare pastry mix according to package directions. Divide into 6 portions and roll each to an 8 1/2 x 5 1/2-inch rectangle. Spoon the ripe olive filling onto half of each rectangle. Beat the egg with 1 tablespoon water, then moisten the edges of dough with egg mixture. Fold the pastry over to enclose filling to make a 5 1/2 x 4 1/4-inch bridie. Seal edges with fork tines. Cut a hole about the size of a quarter in top of each bridie and brush lightly with egg mixture. Place on baking sheet. Bake at 425 degrees for 20 to 25 minutes or until pastry is golden brown. 6 servings.

BABKA

1/2 c. shortening	3 tbsp. milk
1 1/4 c. sifted self-rising	1 egg, beaten
flour	1/2 lb. ground beef

1/3 c. finely chopped onion	1/2 c. finely chopped celery
2 tbsp. butter	1/2 tsp. salt
1 can cream of mushroom soup	

Cut the shortening into the flour, then stir in the milk and egg. Shape into ball and wrap in waxed paper. Chill. Brown the beef and onion in butter and add 3/4 can soup, celery and salt. Divide the pastry in half, then knead and roll out. Fill with half the beef mixture. Roll up as jelly roll. Repeat with remaining dough. Place rolls in a greased pan. Bake at 375 degrees for 25 minutes. Combine remaining soup with 1/4 cup water. Heat and serve over rolls.

Mrs. Bessie A. Bass, Cumberland City, Tennessee

BAKED MEAT LOAF DUMPLINGS

2 1/2 c. flour	3/4 c. shortening
1 tsp. salt	1/4 c. water

Sift the flour with the salt and reserve 1/3 cup of the flour mixture. Cut the shortening into remaining flour. Mix reserved flour mixture with water, then add to shortening mixture. Mix and shape into ball, then divide in half. Roll each half of the dough 1/2 inch thick and cut into 3 squares.

Filling

1 lb. hamburger	1 tsp. salt
1 egg	1/4 tsp. pepper
1/3 c. fine bread crumbs	1/3 c. catsup
2 tbsp. minced onion	Milk

Combine all the ingredients except milk. Place 1/2 cup filling in center of each square. Moisten edges with milk, then bring edges together and pinch to seal. Place in a shallow pan. Bake at 400 degrees for 1 hour. Serve with tomato or creole sauce. 6 servings.

Mrs. Anna Hess, Birmingham, Alabama

BEEF CRUST CASSEROLE

1 1/2 lb. lean ground beef	1 10-oz. package frozen peas
1/2 c. chopped onions	and carrots
2 tsp. salt	1/2 c. converted rice
1/4 c. catsup	1/2 c. water
2 cans cream of mushroom soup	1 c. chow mein noodles

Combine the beef, onions, 1 1/2 teaspoons salt and catsup, then line a 2 1/2-quart casserole with the mixture. Combine the soup, vegetables, rice, water and remaining salt and mix well. Pour into the beef shell. Cover. Bake in 350-degree oven for 1 hour and 15 minutes. Top with noodles and bake, uncovered, for 15 minutes longer. 6 servings.

Mrs. Hill Clark, Lyerly, Georgia

BIEROCKS

1 lb. hamburger	1 tbsp. salt
1 c. chopped onion	1/4 tsp. pepper
4 tbsp. shortening	1/4 tsp. allspice
2 c. shredded cabbage	1 tbsp. flour

Fry the hamburger and onion in shortening in a skillet until partially cooked. Add the cabbage, salt, pepper, allspice and flour and cook over low heat for about 20 minutes, stirring frequently. Remove from heat and cool slightly.

Dough

2 pkg. yeast	1 tsp. salt
2 c. warm water	4 tbsp. sugar
4 tbsp. shortening	6 c. flour

Dissolve the yeast in warm water in a bowl and add shortening, salt and sugar. Add the flour and mix well. Let rise until doubled in bulk. Punch down and let rise again until doubled in bulk. Roll out 1/4 inch thick on floured board and cut in squares. Place 2 tablespoons hamburger mixture on each square and fold over. Seal edges. Place on a greased cookie sheet. Bake at 400 degrees for 15 to 20 minutes. Brush with melted butter, if desired.

Mrs. Robert Yarman, Fort Supply, Oklahoma

CHEESEBURGER PIE

2 c. chopped onions	2 cans tomato soup
1 1/2 c. chopped celery	1 1/2 tbsp. chili powder
3/4 c. chopped green pepper	1 tsp. salt
2 cloves of garlic, minced	1/4 tsp. pepper
Margarine	Cheese pastry for 2-crust pie
2 lb. hamburger	

Brown the onions, celery, green pepper and garlic lightly in a skillet in a small amount of margarine and remove from pan. Add the hamburger and cook, stirring, until lightly browned. Add the soup, chili powder, salt and pepper and the onion mixture and simmer until flavors are well blended, adding small amount of water if needed. Pour into a pastry-lined casserole. Place remaining pastry, lattice-fashion, on top. Bake at 400 degrees for 20 minutes.

Mrs. G. M. Davis, Utica, Mississippi

CHEESE PASTRY PIE

1/2 sm. onion, chopped	1 tsp. salt
3 tbsp. cooking oil	1 No. 2 can tomato juice
1 lb. ground beef	1/2 c. chopped celery
2 tbsp. chopped green pepper	2 tsp. Worcestershire sauce
1/4 c. flour	Cheese Pastry

Saute the onion in oil for 5 minutes, then add the beef and green pepper and brown well. Stir in flour and salt, then add the tomato juice. Cook until thickened, stirring constantly. Add the celery and Worcestershire sauce. Pour into an 8-inch square baking dish. Roll the Cheese Pastry 1/4 inch thick and cut out an 8-inch square. Cover filling with pastry. Cut remaining pastry into 1/2-inch strips and place in lattice design over crust. Bake at 375 degrees for 40 minutes.

Cheese Pastry

1 1/2 c. sifted flour	3/4 c. shredded cheese
1/2 tsp. salt	3 to 4 tbsp. cold water
1/2 c. shortening	

Combine the flour and salt, then cut in the shortening and blend in the cheese. Add the water and mix until dough clings together.

Mrs. Odell Talley, Bell Buckle, Tennessee

PARTY POLENTA

3 lb. ground beef	2 tsp. salt
2 onions, chopped	1/2 tsp. hot sauce
1 1-lb. 13-oz. can tomatoes	1 12-oz. package corn
1 6-oz. can tomato paste	muffin mix
4 tsp. chili powder	1/4 c. grated Parmesan cheese

Saute the beef and onions in a deep saucepan for about 10 minutes or until beef is browned, stirring occasionally. Drain off fat. Pour into a 3-quart casserole. Add the tomatoes, tomato paste, chili powder, salt and hot sauce and mix. Prepare the corn muffin mix according to package directions and spread batter over top of casserole. Sprinkle with cheese. Bake in a 400-degree oven for 35 to 40 minutes or until crust is brown. 12 servings.

Party Polenta (above)

Thrifty Supper Pie (below)

THRIFTY SUPPER PIE

1 c. flour	1 1-lb. can cut Blue Lake
1 1/2 tsp. salt	green beans
1/3 c. shortening	1 1-lb. can whole tomatoes
2 to 3 tbsp. cold milk	1/4 to 1/2 tsp. basil
3 tbsp. cornmeal	1/4 to 1/2 tsp. thyme
1/2 lb. bulk sausage	1/2 bay leaf
1/2 lb. ground beef	1/4 c. cornstarch
3/4 c. chopped onion	1/4 c. water
1 clove of garlic, minced	3/4 c. grated Cheddar cheese

Mix the flour and 1/2 teaspoon salt, then cut in the shortening until the consistency of coarse meal. Mix in milk gradually until mixture holds together in a ball. Knead until smooth. Roll out on pastry cloth sprinkled with 2 tablespoons cornmeal to fit into 9-inch pie pan. Fit into pan, then flute a high edge and sprinkle with remaining cornmeal. Bake on lowest shelf of oven at 450 degrees for 15 minutes. Brown the sausage, then drain well. Add the beef and brown. Add the onion and garlic and cook until tender-crisp. Mix in the beans, tomatoes, remaining salt, basil, thyme and bay leaf. Bring to a boil, then cover and simmer for 15 minutes. Discard the bay leaf. Blend the cornstarch with water, then stir into the hot mixture and cook until thickened. Turn into the baked shell and sprinkle with the cheese. Return to oven and bake until cheese melts. Cool for 10 minutes before cutting. 6 servings.

CHEESY BEEF-RICE PIE

1 1/4 lb. ground beef	1 1/4 c. instant rice
1 tbsp. minced onion	2 8-oz. cans tomato sauce
1/4 tsp. salt	1 c. water
Dash of pepper	1/4 c. grated Cheddar cheese

Combine the ground beef, onion, salt and pepper and pat into a 9-inch pie pan forming a crust. Combine the rice, tomato sauce and water and pour into the beef crust. Cover with aluminum foil. Bake at 325 degrees for 30 minutes. Remove the foil and top with cheese. Bake for 10 minutes longer or until cheese is melted. Cut into wedges. 6 servings.

Mrs. Lorraine Felder, Chattanooga, Tennessee

BEEF AND CORN BREAD SUPPER

1 1/2 lb. ground round steak	2 tsp. baking powder
1 can cream of asparagus soup	1 tsp. salt
1/4 c. finely chopped onion	1/4 c. oil
2 tsp. Worcestershire sauce	2/3 c. milk
3/4 c. sifted flour	6 green pepper rings
1/2 c. cornmeal	

Preheat oven to 400 degrees. Brown the ground steak in a skillet. Add the soup, onion and Worcestershire sauce and simmer for 5 minutes. Sift the flour, cornmeal, baking powder and salt together into a medium bowl. Add the oil and milk and beat until smooth. Pour over beef mixture in skillet and spread to edge. Top with green pepper rings. Bake for 15 to 20 minutes or until brown.

Mrs. Estell Shalla, Bay City, Texas

CHILI BAKE WITH CORN BREAD TOPPING

2 tbsp. shortening	1 c. cooked kidney beans
1 sm. onion, chopped	2 tsp. salt
1 sm. green pepper, chopped	1 1/2 tsp. chili powder
1 lb. ground beef	1/4 tsp. pepper
1 No. 2 can tomatoes	

Melt the shortening in a large skillet. Add the onion, green pepper and beef and brown lightly. Drain 1/2 cup liquid from tomatoes. Add remaining tomatoes and liquid to skillet. Add the kidney beans, salt, chili powder and pepper and mix well. Pour into a 2-quart casserole.

Corn Bread Topping

3 tbsp. melted shortening	1 tsp. sugar
1/2 c. milk	1 c. self-rising cornmeal
1 egg, beaten	1/2 c. sifted self-rising flour

Add the shortening and milk to egg in a bowl. Stir in the sugar, cornmeal and flour and drop by spoonfuls on top of beef mixture. Bake at 400 degrees for 25 minutes or until brown. 6 servings.

Mrs. Lewis Beazley, Terry, Mississippi

BURGER UPSIDE-DOWN CORN BREAD

2 tbsp. butter or margarine	1/4 c. sliced ripe olives
1 c. minced onion	1 8-oz. can tomato puree
1 1/2 lb. ground chuck	1 tbsp. flour
1 tsp. chili powder	1 12-oz. package corn muffin
1 tsp. salt	mix
1/8 tsp. pepper	1 tbsp. minced parsley

Melt the butter in a large skillet. Add the onion and saute for about 5 minutes or until golden brown. Add the ground chuck and cook over medium heat, stirring frequently, for about 5 minutes or until browned. Add the chili powder, salt, pepper, olives and tomato puree and simmer for 5 minutes longer. Combine the flour and 1 tablespoon water and stir until smooth. Add to beef mixture and cook, stirring constantly, for 3 minutes or until thickened. Place in a 9 x 9 x 1-inch baking pan. Prepare corn muffin mix according to package directions and spread over beef mixture. Bake in 400-degree oven for 20 minutes. Invert on a serving platter and garnish with parsley.

Mrs. Nell White, Miami, Florida

CHILI CON CARNE PIE

1/2 c. cornmeal	1 lb. hamburger
1/2 c. flour	1 sm. onion, chopped
2 tsp. baking powder	1 16-oz. can tomatoes
1/4 tsp. salt	1 sm. can tomato sauce
1 egg	1 16-oz. can chili beans
1/2 c. milk	1 tsp. chili powder
4 tbsp. melted shortening	

Mix the cornmeal, flour, baking powder and salt in a bowl. Add egg and milk and beat thoroughly. Add 2 tablespoons shortening and stir until mixed. Pour 3/4 of the mixture into a greased 8-inch square baking dish. Cook the hamburger and onion in remaining shortening in a skillet until brown. Add tomatoes, tomato sauce, chili beans and chili powder and simmer for 20 minutes. Place over cornmeal mixture in baking dish and top with remaining cornmeal mixture. Bake in 375-degree oven for 25 to 30 minutes. 4 servings.

Linda Maye, Richmond, Virginia

CORN BREAD AND MEATBALL RING

1 recipe corn bread batter	3/4 c. rolled oats
1 1/2 lb. ground beef	1 No. 2 can tomatoes
1/4 c. chopped onion	Shortening
2 tsp. salt	1 6-oz. can tomato paste
1/4 tsp. pepper	1/3 c. chopped green pepper

Pour the batter into a well-greased 1 1/2-quart ring mold. Bake at 425 degrees for 20 to 25 minutes. Combine the ground beef, onion, salt, pepper and oats.

Drain the tomatoes and reserve tomato juice. Add the reserved tomato juice to the ground beef mixture and mix well. Shape into small balls and brown in small amount of shortening in a skillet. Cover and cook over low heat for about 30 minutes. Combine the tomatoes, tomato paste and green pepper in a saucepan and cook over low heat until thickened. Place the corn bread on a serving plate. Place the meatballs in center of corn bread ring and pour tomato sauce over meatballs.

Maybelle Ferrell, Dunnellon, Florida

EUNICE'S MEAT AND CORN BREAD PIE

3 tbsp. margarine	1 tsp. salt
1 lge. onion, chopped fine	1/8 tsp. pepper
1 lb. ground round steak	1 can cream of mushroom soup
2 tbsp. flour	1 No. 303 can small green peas

Melt the margarine in a large, heavy frying pan. Add the onion and saute over low heat for 10 minutes. Add the ground round and cook over medium heat until brown, breaking up ground round. Blend in flour, salt and pepper. Stir in the soup and peas and cook for 1 minute. Pour into a 3-quart baking dish.

Corn Bread Topping

1 c. (scant) cornmeal	1/2 tsp. salt
1 tbsp. flour	1/3 c. milk
1 tbsp. sugar	1 egg, slightly beaten
1 1/2 tsp. baking powder	1 tbsp. salad oil

Sift the cornmeal, flour, sugar, baking powder and salt together into a medium bowl. Stir in the milk, egg and oil. Spoon over beef mixture. Bake at 400 degrees for 20 to 25 minutes or until brown. 4 servings.

Mrs. Sidney Chancler, Tulsa, Oklahoma

CORN BREAD AND GRAVY PIE

1/2 lb. ground beef	1 1/8 tsp. salt
1/2 lb. pork sausage	3 tbsp. chopped green peppers
2 tbsp. chopped onion	1 recipe corn bread batter
6 tbsp. flour	1 c. tomatoes

Brown the meats and onion in a skillet. Drain off excess fat and reserve. Blend in 4 tablespoons flour and 1 teaspoon salt and add green peppers. Spread in a baking pan and pour corn bread batter over beef mixture. Bake at 375 degrees for 35 to 40 minutes. Invert onto a serving platter. Brown remaining flour in reserved fat in a saucepan. Add tomatoes and remaining salt and simmer for 5 minutes. Serve with pie.

Gertie Stapp, Loudon, Tennessee

BEEF AND CORNMEAL PIE

1/4 c. flour	2 tbsp. chopped green pepper
1/2 c. cornmeal	1 med. onion, chopped
2 tsp. baking powder	2 tbsp. bacon drippings
2 1/2 tsp. salt	2 tsp. chili powder
1 tsp. sugar	1/2 c. tomato juice
1 egg, slightly beaten	1/2 c. cooked rice
1/2 c. milk	4 green pepper rings
3 tbsp. melted margarine	4 sm. cubes cheese
3/4 lb. hamburger	Grated cheese
2 tbsp. chopped celery	

Sift the flour, cornmeal, baking powder, 1/2 teaspoon salt and sugar together into a bowl. Mix the egg and milk. Add egg mixture and margarine to sifted ingredients and mix. Reserve 4 tablespoons batter. Pour remaining batter into a greased 9-inch pie plate. Cook the hamburger, celery, chopped green pepper and onion in bacon drippings in a skillet until brown. Add remaining salt, chili powder, tomato juice and rice and spoon over batter carefully. Place green pepper rings over beef mixture and fill each ring with 1 tablespoon reserved batter. Place 1 cube cheese in each green pepper ring. Cover top with grated cheese. Bake at 400 degrees for 35 minutes.

Mrs. Mary K. Schulman, St. Petersburg, Florida

CORN MUFFIN-BEEF PIE

1 can consomme	1/8 tsp. pepper
1 1/2 lb. ground beef	2 tbsp. steak sauce
1 tbsp. chopped onion	1 pkg. corn muffin mix
1 tsp. salt	

Mix all ingredients except corn muffin mix and spread in a 10-inch cake pan. Prepare corn muffin mix according to package directions and spread over beef mixture. Bake at 350 degrees for 30 minutes. 6 servings.

Mrs. Mabel Shade, Morganton, North Carolina

CORN PONE PIE

1 lb. ground beef	1 sm. onion, minced
1 sm. can spaghetti in tomato sauce	1 tsp. celery salt
1 No. 303 can kidney beans	1/8 tsp. pepper
2 c. canned tomatoes and juice	1 14-oz. bottle catsup
1 green pepper, chopped	Corn Bread Topping

Cook the ground beef in a skillet over moderate heat, stirring, until browned, then pour off fat. Add spaghetti, beans and tomatoes and mix. Stir in remaining ingredients except Corn Bread Topping. Turn into 2-quart casserole and cover with Corn Bread Topping. Bake at 400 degrees for 30 to 40 minutes.

Corn Bread Topping

3/4 c. cornmeal	1 tsp. soda
1 c. buttermilk	1 egg, beaten
1 tsp. salt	

Combine all ingredients in a bowl and mix well.

Mrs. Loyd Frye, Henderson, Tennessee

HAMBURGER-CORN PONE PIE

1 lb. ground beef	1 tsp. Worcestershire sauce
1/3 c. chopped onion	1 c. canned tomatoes
1 tbsp. shortening	1 c. kidney beans, drained
2 tsp. chili powder	1 c. corn bread batter
3/4 tsp. salt	

Brown the beef and onion in shortening in a skillet. Add the chili powder, salt, Worcestershire sauce and tomatoes and cover. Simmer for 15 minutes, then add kidney beans. Pour the beef mixture into a 1 1/2-quart casserole and top with the corn bread batter. Bake at 425 degrees until corn bread is brown.

Mrs. Richard Arnold, Phillips, Texas

HAMBURGER UPSIDE-DOWN PIE

2 tbsp. salad oil	1 8-oz. can tomato sauce
1 med. onion, minced	1 tsp. salt
1/2 c. chopped green pepper	1/4 tsp. pepper
1 lb. hamburger	2 tbsp. catsup

Heat the oil in a skillet. Add the onion, green pepper and hamburger and cook until brown. Add the tomato sauce, salt, pepper and catsup and turn into a 2-quart casserole.

Topping

1/2 c. sifted flour	3/4 c. yellow cornmeal
2 tsp. baking powder	1 egg, beaten
1 tsp. salt	1/2 c. milk
1 tbsp. sugar	2 tbsp. salad oil

Sift the flour, baking powder, salt and sugar together into a mixing bowl. Add the cornmeal. Combine the egg, milk and salad oil. Add to flour mixture and stir until dry ingredients are moistened. Spread over hamburger mixture. Bake at 425 degrees for about 25 minutes or until done. Invert onto a serving plate and cut in wedges. 6-8 servings.

Vera Hobson, Baltimore, Maryland

JALAPENO-HAMBURGER PIE

1 lb. ground beef	1 c. chopped onion
1/2 lb. ground pork	1 1/2 tsp. salt
1 tbsp. oil	1 tbsp. chopped parsley
1 c. chopped bell pepper	2 tbsp. barbecue sauce
1 c. chopped celery	Dash of pepper

Brown the meats in oil in a skillet, then stir in remaining ingredients.

Corn Bread Topping

1 6-oz. can jalapeno peppers	4 tsp. sugar
2 eggs, beaten	1 med. onion, chopped
1 c. milk	1 c. grated sharp Cheddar
1 1/2 c. corn bread mix	cheese
1/4 c. flour	1 can cream-style corn
1/4 c. cooking oil	

Drain and chop the jalapeno peppers. Place in a bowl. Add remaining ingredients and mix well. Pour over meat mixture. Bake at 350 degrees for 1 hour. Invert on a serving platter. 8 servings.

Robin Ann Lester, Lewisville, Texas

ONE-DISH PIE

1 can green peas	1/2 c. water
1 can whole kernel corn	1/4 c. melted butter
Salt and pepper to taste	1 1/2 c. self-rising cornmeal
1 can tomato paste	1/2 c. self-rising flour
1/2 c. chopped onions	1 egg
1/2 c. chopped green pepper	1/2 c. milk
1 lb. ground beef	1/2 c. water
1 can tomatoes	

Drain the peas and corn and reserve liquid. Place the peas and corn in a greased 2-quart casserole and sprinkle with salt and pepper. Add the tomato paste, onions and green pepper. Mix reserved liquid with enough water to make 1 1/2 cups liquid. Add to casserole and mix well. Season the ground beef with salt and pepper and place over corn mixture. Add the tomatoes, water and butter. Mix the cornmeal and flour with egg. Add the milk and water and mix well. Pour over casserole. Bake at 300 degrees for 1 hour.

Tommie Simpson, Millry, Alabama

PEPPER AND BEEF OVER CORN BREAD

Green pepper rings	1 8-oz. can tomato sauce
1/2 c. chopped onion	1 1/2 tsp. chili powder
1 lb. ground beef	1 tsp. salt
1 tbsp. shortening	1/4 tsp. pepper

Arrange green pepper rings in bottom of a baking pan. Cook the onion and ground beef in shortening in a skillet until brown. Add the tomato sauce and seasonings and simmer for about 5 minutes. Pour over green pepper rings.

Corn Bread Batter

1 c. flour	1 egg
1 c. cornmeal	1 c. milk
4 tsp. baking powder	1/4 c. melted shortening
1/2 tsp. salt	

Combine the flour, cornmeal, baking powder and salt in a bowl. Stir in remaining ingredients and pour over beef mixture. Bake at 425 degrees for 20 to 25 minutes. Invert onto a platter.

Mrs. C. B. Hodges, Louisville, Kentucky

MEAT-ZA PIE

1 lb. ground beef	1 2-oz. can sliced mushrooms
1/2 to 1 tsp. garlic salt	2 to 3 slices Cheddar cheese,
1/2 c. fine dry bread crumbs	cut into strips
2/3 c. evaporated milk	1/4 tsp. oregano, crumbled
1/3 c. catsup	2 tbsp. grated Parmesan cheese

Preheat oven to 400 degrees. Place the beef, garlic salt and crumbs in a 9-inch pie pan, then add the milk and mix with a fork. Spread the mixture evenly over bottom of pan, then form a low rim around edge. Spread catsup over the beef mixture to the rim. Arrange mushrooms on top. Place cheese strips in crisscross pattern over top. Sprinkle with oregano and Parmesan cheese. Bake for 20 minutes or until cheese is melted and lightly browned. Cut in wedges to serve. 4 servings.

Meat-Za Pie (above)

BEEF-BISCUIT ROLL

1/2 c. chopped onion	1/8 tsp. pepper
1/2 c. chopped green pepper	1 recipe biscuit dough
1 lb. ground beef	Butter
1/2 tsp. salt	

Brown the onion, green pepper and beef in a small amount of fat in a frying pan, then add salt and pepper. Roll out dough, 1/4 inch thick, then spread with beef mixture. Roll as for jelly roll and chill. Cut in 1 1/2-inch slices. Place in greased pan, cut side up, and brush with melted butter. Bake for 20 to 25 minutes at 450 degrees. Serve with brown gravy, cheese sauce or creamed peas. 5-6 servings.

Mrs. Mary Young, Pensacola, Florida

MEAT SQUARE

2 tbsp. chopped onion	1/2 tsp. pepper
1 c. ground beef	3/4 c. tomato soup
1/2 tsp. salt	1 1/4 c. cooked green beans

Brown the onion in 1 tablespoon fat, then add the beef, salt and pepper. Cook for 5 minutes. Add the tomato soup and beans and mix well. Pour in an 8-inch square pan.

Drop Biscuits

1 c. flour	1/4 c. cooking oil
1 1/2 tsp. baking powder	1/2 c. milk
1/2 tsp. salt	

Combine the dry ingredients, then combine the oil and milk. Pour the milk mixture into flour mixture all at once and stir until mixed. Drop from a spoon onto the beef mixture and spread to edge of pan. Bake at 450 degrees for 25 minutes.

Mrs. Mose Rash, Crewe, Virginia

TACO PINWHEELS

1 lb. ground beef	1/4 c. cornmeal
1 15 3/4-oz. can chili beans	3/4 c. shredded Cheddar cheese
2 tbsp. onion flakes	1/2 c. crushed corn chips
2 1/4 tsp. chili powder	1 15-oz. can tomato sauce
1 to 2 tsp. garlic salt	with bits
1 can lge.-sized refrigerator	2 tbsp. chopped green pepper
flaky or buttermilk flaky	Dash of hot sauce (opt.)
biscuits	

Brown the ground beef in a large skillet and drain. Mash the beans, then add the onion flakes, 2 teaspoons chili powder and garlic salt and mix well. Stir into the ground beef. Separate the biscuit dough into 10 biscuits. Sprinkle the cornmeal on working surface, then place 2 rows of 5 biscuits each together and press to form 1 piece of dough. Roll to form an 8 x 16-inch rectangle, then spread the beef mixture over dough. Roll up jelly roll fashion, starting at 16-inch side. Cut into 10 slices. Place slices, cut side down, forming 2 rows in a greased 13 x 9-inch baking dish. Sprinkle with the cheese and corn chips. Bake at 350 degrees for 35 to 40 minutes or until pinwheels are light golden brown. Combine the remaining ingredients and remaining chili powder in a saucepan and bring to a boil. Simmer, uncovered, for 5 minutes, stirring frequently. Serve over the pinwheels. 10 servings.

Photograph for this recipe on page 130.

PIRATE'S PIE

2 lb. lean ground beef	2 c. canned kidney beans,
1 onion, chopped	drained
1 green pepper, chopped	1 tbsp. angostura aromatic
2 tbsp. shortening	bitters
2 c. canned tomatoes	1 12-oz. package corn
1 1/2 tsp. salt	muffin mix
1/3 c. chopped pimento	

Brown the beef, onion and green pepper in melted shortening, then add the tomatoes and salt. Cover and simmer for 15 minutes. Stir in the pimento, kidney beans and angostura bitters and heat through. Pour into greased 2-quart baking dish. Prepare corn muffin mix according to package directions for dumplings. Spoon dumplings close together, around edge of casserole, to form solid border. Bake at 425 degrees for 15 to 20 minutes. 6-8 servings.

Pirate's Pie (above)

HAMBURGER-BISCUIT BAKE

2 c. flour	1 lb. ground beef
3 tsp. baking powder	1/4 c. minced onion
1 3/4 tsp. salt	1/2 tsp. hamburger seasoning
1/2 c. shortening	1/4 tsp. pepper
1 egg, lightly beaten	1 tbsp. prepared mustard
1/3 c. milk	1/4 c. chili sauce

Sift the flour, baking powder and 3/4 teaspoon salt together, then cut in the shortening. Add egg and milk and mix well. Roll out into two 8-inch squares. Brown the beef and onion in 1 tablespoon hot fat. Add the remaining salt and remaining ingredients. Place dough in 8-inch square pan and pour in the beef mixture. Top with remaining dough. Bake at 425 degrees for 25 minutes. Cut into squares.

Parsley Sauce

3 tbsp. butter	2 tbsp. minced parsley
3 tbsp. flour	1/2 tsp. celery salt
3/4 tsp. salt	1 tsp. Worcestershire sauce
1/8 tsp. pepper	1 1/2 c. milk

Melt the butter in a saucepan, then stir in the flour and seasonings. Add the milk gradually and cook, stirring constantly, until thickened.

Mrs. June W. Galford, Dunmore, West Virginia

TOMATO-HAMBURGER PIE

1/4 c. chopped onion	1/4 tsp. pepper
4 tbsp. corn oil	1 c. sifted flour
1 lb. ground beef	1 1/2 tsp. baking powder
1/4 c. catsup	1/3 c. milk
1 tbsp. pickle relish	Tomato Sauce
1 1/2 tsp. salt	

Preheat the oven to 425 degrees. Saute the onion in 2 tablespoons corn oil until transparent, then add the ground beef and brown. Pour off the excess fat, then add the catsup, relish, 1 teaspoon salt and the pepper and blend. Simmer until heated through. Sift the flour, baking powder and remaining salt together, then add the milk and remaining oil and stir until blended. Knead for 10 to 15 times in a bowl, then roll between waxed paper into a 12-inch circle. Remove the top paper and invert dough into lightly oiled 9-inch pie pan, then peel off paper. Fit into pan loosely, then fold edge under. Add the beef mixture. Spread the Tomato Sauce over the top. Bake for 25 minutes.

Tomato Sauce

1 8-oz. can tomato sauce	2 tbsp. chopped onion
2 tbsp. chopped green pepper	Salt and pepper to taste

Blend the tomato sauce with the green pepper and onion, then season with salt and pepper.

HAMBURGER SKILLET PIE WITH SCONE BISCUIT TOPPING

1 1/2 c. sifted flour	1/3 c. corn oil
2 tsp. baking powder	1/3 c. milk
1 tsp. salt	1 egg, beaten

Preheat oven to 425 degrees. Sift the flour, baking powder and salt together into a bowl, then add the oil, milk, and egg and stir just until blended. Roll between waxed paper into a 7 x 11-inch rectangle.

Filling

1 lb. ground beef	1/4 c. chopped green pepper
1 tbsp. corn oil	1/2 c. chopped onion
1/4 c. flour	1 c. diced celery
2 tsp. salt	4 oz. American cheese,
1/4 tsp. pepper	grated
2 c. tomato juice	

Brown the ground beef in corn oil in a large skillet, then drain off the excess fat. Stir in the flour, salt, pepper and tomato juice, then add the green pepper, onion and celery. Bring to a boil, stirring constantly. Pour into a 7 x 11-inch baking dish. Place biscuit topping over hot mixture. Bake for 25 to 30 minutes or until topping is golden brown. Remove from oven and sprinkle crust with cheese. 4-6 servings.

Hamburger Skillet Pie with Scone Biscuit Topping (above)
Tomato-Hamburger Pie (page 146)

STROGANOFF PIE

1 1/2 lb. ground beef	1 7-oz. can mushrooms,
2 tbsp. instant minced onion	drained
1 tbsp. parsley flakes	1 can vegetable soup
1/4 tsp. garlic powder	1 c. sour cream
1 tsp. salt	1/2 c. milk
1/2 tsp. pepper	

Place the beef, onion, parsley and garlic powder in skillet and saute until browned. Stir in the salt, pepper, mushrooms and soup and simmer for 15 minutes. Blend in the sour cream and milk and heat thoroughly. Place in 9 x 9-inch baking dish.

Biscuit Topping

1 1/2 c. sifted flour	1/4 tsp. pepper
2 tsp. baking powder	1/4 c. shortening
1 tsp. paprika	3/4 c. milk
1/2 tsp. salt	1 tsp. poppy seed
1/2 tsp. celery seed	

Combine the first 6 ingredients and cut in the shortening. Stir in the milk. Drop by spoonfuls onto beef mixture and sprinkle with poppy seed. Bake at 425 degrees for 15 to 20 minutes.

Mrs. W. J. Grichar, Bremond, Texas

INDIVIDUAL PIZZA PIES

2 cans tomato paste	1/2 tsp. thyme
1 tsp. salt	2 cans refrigerator biscuits
1 tsp. Worcestershire sauce	1 lb. ground beef
1 tsp. garlic salt	1 1/2 to 2 c. grated cheese
4 to 6 drops of hot sauce	Oregano to taste

Combine the tomato paste, salt, Worcestershire sauce, garlic salt, hot sauce and thyme. Roll each biscuit on a floured board to a 4-inch circle and cover each with a thin layer of beef, tomato paste mixture, grated cheese and oregano. Place on an ungreased cookie sheet. Bake at 425 degrees for 10 minutes. Yield: 20 servings.

Mrs. Leo Howerton, Carlsbad, New Mexico

PEASANT'S COULIBAC

Meat Loaf Mixture	1 1/2 tsp. sugar
1 1/4 to 1 3/4 c. flour	3/4 tsp. salt

| 1 pkg. yeast | 1 tbsp. peanut oil |
| 1/2 c. hot water | 1 egg, beaten |

Shape Meat Loaf Mixture into a loaf and place in 9 x 5 x 3-inch loaf pan. Bake at 375 degrees for 1 hour or until done. Remove from pan and set aside to cool or refrigerate overnight. Mix 1/2 cup flour, sugar, salt and dry yeast thoroughly in a small bowl. Add hot water and oil gradually to dry ingredients and beat for 1 minute at medium speed of electric mixer, scraping bowl occasionally. Beat at high speed for 1 minute longer, scraping bowl occasionally. Stir in enough additional flour to make a soft dough. Turn out onto lightly floured board and knead for about 8 to 10 minutes or until smooth and elastic. Place in greased bowl, turning to grease top. Cover and let rise in warm place, free from draft, for about 30 minutes or until doubled in bulk. Punch down dough and turn out onto lightly floured board. Roll into a 12 x 15-inch rectangle. Line a well-greased 9 x 5 x 3-inch loaf pan with dough. Place baked meat loaf in pan and cover with dough. Seal edges well. Brush with egg. Bake at 375 degrees for 30 minutes. Remove the loaf from pan and invert onto baking sheet, then brush with egg. Bake for 10 minutes longer or until golden brown. Cool slightly, then cut into slices and serve.

Meat Loaf Mixture

1 lb. ground beef chuck	1 tbsp. chopped parsley
1/2 lb. ground pork	1 med. clove of garlic,
1/2 lb. ground veal	minced
1 c. fine dry bread crumbs	2 tsp. salt
3/4 c. chopped onion	1/4 tsp. pepper
2 eggs	

Combine all the ingredients and mix well.

Peasant's Coulibac (page 148)

CHEDDAR PIZZA

1 pkg. yeast	1 tsp. salt
1/4 c. warm water	1 tbsp. sugar
1 c. milk, scalded	3 c. sifted flour
1 1/2 tbsp. shortening	

Dissolve the yeast in the warm water. Mix the milk, shortening, salt and sugar in a bowl and cool to lukewarm. Add the yeast and mix well. Add enough flour to make a stiff dough and mix thoroughly. Turn out on a floured board and knead for 5 to 10 minutes. Place in a greased bowl and turn to grease surface. Cover with a towel. Let rise in a warm place until doubled in bulk, then punch down. Cover and let rise until doubled in bulk. Turn out on a floured board and divide in half. Cover and let rest for 10 minutes. Roll each half out to a 12-inch circle and place on 2 greased pizza pans or cookie sheets. Shape edge into a ridge.

Filling

2 lb. ground beef	2 tsp. basil
2 med. onions, minced	2 tsp. oregano
1 to 2 tsp. salt	2 8-oz. cans tomato sauce
1/2 tsp. pepper	2 c. grated Cheddar or
1/2 tsp. garlic salt (opt.)	mozzarella cheese

Brown the beef in a large frying pan. Add the onions and cook over medium heat until onions are transparent. Add seasonings and mix well. Place half the beef mixture on each circle of dough. Add tomato sauce and sprinkle cheese on top. Bake at 375 degrees for 20 to 25 minutes or until crust is golden brown. 12 servings.

Mrs. L. A. Cross, Oklahoma City, Oklahoma

HAMBURGER CRUST PIE

2 lb. hamburger	2 pkg. frozen French fries
Salt and pepper to taste	1 can cream of chicken soup
2 tsp. chopped onion	1 can cream of mushroom soup

Press the hamburger into bottom of a 9-inch square pan and add salt, pepper and onion. Arrange the French fries over hamburger and spread soups over French fries. Bake at 350 degrees for 1 hour. Cut into squares to serve. 8 servings.

Martha Nichols, Raleigh, North Carolina

SHEPHERD'S PIE

3 tbsp. diced onion	1/4 tsp. salt
3 tbsp. diced green pepper	1 can beef soup with vegetables
2 tbsp. butter	1 c. mashed potatoes
1 c. ground beef	Grated cheese (opt.)

Cook the onion and green pepper in butter in a skillet until tender. Add the beef and cook until brown. Sprinkle with salt. Add soup and simmer for 5 minutes, stirring occasionally. Place in a casserole and top with potatoes. Bake in 400-

Beef Pies

degree oven for 20 minutes or until potatoes are brown. Cover with cheese and bake until cheese is melted. 4 servings.

Mrs. W. K. Templeton, Kernersville, North Carolina

HAMBURGER SHORTCAKE

2 c. sifted flour	1 lb. ground beef
3 tsp. baking powder	1/4 c. catsup
2 tsp. salt	1 tbsp. pickle relish
Corn oil	1/4 tsp. pepper
2/3 c. milk	1 tbsp. chopped pimento
1/4 c. chopped onion	Tomato Sauce

Preheat the oven to 425 degrees. Sift the flour with the baking powder and 1 teaspoon salt. Pour 1/3 cup corn oil and milk into measuring cup, but do not stir, then pour all at once into flour. Stir with a fork until mixture leaves side of bowl. Knead 10 times without additional flour. Roll between waxed paper into an 8 x 12-inch rectangle. Saute the onion in 2 tablespoons oil until golden, then add the beef and brown. Stir in catsup, pickle relish, remaining salt, pepper and pimento, then remove from the heat. Spread over biscuit dough. Roll as for a jelly roll and place in 9 x 13-inch pan. Bake for about 25 minutes or until golden brown. Serve with hot Tomato Sauce.

Tomato Sauce

2 tbsp. chopped onion	1 8-oz. can tomato sauce
2 tbsp. chopped green pepper	Salt and pepper to taste
1 tbsp. corn oil	

Saute the onion and green pepper in oil until onion is transparent, then add the tomato sauce and salt and pepper. Simmer until heated through.

Hamburger Shortcake (above)

Shanghai Casserole (page 154)

specialty & quantity dishes

Because of its adaptability, ground beef is a popular ingredient in many specialty dishes. And because of its low cost, it is often the basis of quantity cooking – the creation of dishes which serve crowds ranging in size from twenty-five or fifty to several hundred people.

This section brings together the very best specialty and quantity recipes from kitchens throughout the Southland. Discover the secret of preparing fabulous Hamburger Shish Kabobs . . . Sour Cream-Beef Casserole . . . or Beef Stuffed Peppers. Serve one of these elegant specialty dishes to your family and friends – it's such dishes that will mark you as a truly great cook!

And the next time your church or civic group is planning a cookout or supper for a crowd, why not offer to provide some of the food. Think how your friends will marvel as you effortlessly prepare Camp Stew for Two Hundred . . . Barbecued Hamburger for a Crowd of Fifty . . . Lasagna for Fifty . . . or Party Pizza Quickies for Twenty-Four. You can depend upon these recipes – they've been tested and proven in homes and communities throughout the South. They're favorites of the women who prepared them, and they're certain to become your favorites, too. Explore these pages now . . . and discover the excitement of ground beef specialty and quantity cooking!

SHANGHAI CASSEROLE

1 lb. lean ground beef	1 can cream of mushroom soup
1 tsp. onion powder	3 c. cooked rice
1 tsp. garlic powder	2 tbsp. soy sauce
1 c. sliced celery	1/4 tsp. pepper
1 c. cooked mixed vegetables	1 c. Chinese noodles

Brown the beef with the onion and garlic powders in a lightly greased skillet. Add the celery, mixed vegetables and soup, then stir in the rice and seasonings. Turn into a greased 2-quart casserole and cover. Bake at 350 degrees for 25 minutes. Remove the cover and top with the noodles. Bake, uncovered, for 5 minutes longer. 6 servings.

Photograph for this recipe on page 152.

BAKED SPAGHETTI

1 sm. bottle stuffed olives	1 can tomato soup
1 onion, minced	2 sm. cans mushrooms
1 tbsp. margarine	Salt and pepper to taste
1 lb. ground round steak	1 8-oz. package thin spaghetti
1 med. green pepper, chopped	1/2 lb. sharp cheese, grated
3 stalks celery, chopped	1 can cream of mushroom soup

Drain the olives and reserve liquid. Brown the onion in margarine in a skillet. Add the ground steak, green pepper, celery, tomato soup, reserved olive liquid, mushrooms and liquid, salt and pepper. Break the spaghetti into short lengths and cook according to package directions. Place alternate layers of spaghetti, beef sauce and grated cheese in a casserole and top with mushroom soup. Bake at 325 degrees for 45 minutes. Slice the olives and place on top of casserole. 8-10 servings.

Mrs. Bose Ethridge, Anderson, South Carolina

FRENCH MEAT ROLL

3/4 lb. ground beef	1 tsp. salt
1/2 c. chopped celery	2 c. prepared biscuit mix
2 eggs, beaten	1 tsp. parsley flakes
1/3 c. chopped onion	1 tsp. dry mustard
1 tbsp. Worcestershire sauce	1 can celery soup
1/4 c. catsup	1/2 soup can milk
1/4 c. rolled oats	

Combine first 8 ingredients and mix. Prepare the biscuit mix according to package directions, adding the parsley and mustard. Roll out into a 10 x 12-inch rectangle. Spread with the ground beef mixture and roll as for jelly roll. Place on a cookie sheet. Bake in 375-degree oven for 35 to 40 minutes. Mix the soup with the milk in a saucepan and heat through. Serve with the Meat Roll.

Mrs. H. G. Vaughn, Morristown, Tennessee

EGGPLANT ROMANO

1 lb. ground beef	1/4 tsp. basil
Olive oil	Salt and pepper to taste
1/2 onion, chopped	4 cans tomato sauce
1/2 green pepper, chopped	1/2 tsp. sugar
1 clove of garlic, crushed	1 eggplant
1 tsp. garlic salt	Flour
1/4 tsp. oregano	3 eggs, beaten
1/4 tsp. thyme	1/3 c. grated Romano cheese

Brown the ground beef in small amount of olive oil in a skillet. Add the onion, green pepper, garlic, garlic salt, herbs, salt and pepper and cook until onion is tender. Add the tomato sauce and sugar and simmer for 45 minutes. Peel the eggplant and slice thin. Sprinkle with salt and dredge with flour. Dip in eggs. Brown in small amount of olive oil, drain well and place in a casserole. Top with ground beef mixture and sprinkle with cheese. Bake at 350 degrees for 40 minutes. 6 servings.

Mrs. E. C. Grasty, Casa Grande, Arizona

AVOCADO HALF SHELLS WITH TARTARE STEAK

1 lb. twice ground sirloin or round of beef	2 lge. ripe California avocados
1/4 c. minced onion	Lemon juice
2 tbsp. chopped parsley	4 egg yolks (opt.)
3/4 tsp. salt	Capers

Mix the beef, onion, parsley and salt together. Cut the avocados in half lengthwise, twisting gently to separate halves. Whack a sharp knife directly into seeds and twist to lift out. Brush the avocados with lemon juice then fill with the beef mixture. Make indentation in centers, then add egg yolks. Sprinkle with capers. Serve or garnish with Worcestershire sauce, hot sauce or lemon wedges. 4 servings.

Avocado Half Shells with Tartare Steak (above)

155

CHINESE EGG ROLLS

1 lb. ground beef	2 c. bean sprouts
1/4 c. butter	2 tsp. salt
4 c. shredded cabbage	Flour
1/2 c. diced celery	2 tbsp. cornstarch
1/4 c. soy sauce	1 egg
Sugar	Oil
1/2 c. finely chopped onion	Hot mustard

Brown the ground beef in butter in a skillet. Add the cabbage, celery, soy sauce, 2 tablespoons sugar, onion, bean sprouts and 1 teaspoon salt and cook for 5 minutes. Drain and cool. Sift 2 cups flour, remaining salt and cornstarch together into a bowl. Beat the egg with 1 teaspoon sugar and add to the flour mixture. Add 2 cups water gradually, stirring constantly, and beat until smooth. Grease a 6-inch skillet lightly with oil. Pour about 4 tablespoons batter into skillet and tilt pan to spread batter over entire surface. Cook until edges pull away from side of skillet and remove from skillet. Place about 1 tablespoon ground beef mixture in center and fold edges in. Mix 1 tablespoon flour and 2 tablespoons water and seal the egg roll. Repeat with remaining batter and ground beef mixture. Fry rolls in deep hot fat until brown and spread with mustard sparingly. 30-40 egg rolls.

Mrs. A. E. Pooser, Jr., Waycross, Georgia

LEMON MEATBALLS

1 c. bread crumbs	1/4 c. chopped green peppers
1/3 c. catsup	2 tbsp. chopped onion
1 egg, slightly beaten	1/4 c. lemon juice
1 lb. ground beef	1 tsp. salt
1 c. grated cheese	12 slices bacon

Mix the bread crumbs, catsup and egg. Combine with remaining ingredients except bacon. Mix well and shape into 12 balls. Wrap each ball with 1 strip bacon and secure with toothpicks. Place on shallow rack in a baking pan. Bake in 400-degree oven for 45 minutes or until bacon is done, turning meatballs several times to cook bacon evenly. 4 servings.

Mrs. Lee Stringfield, Cottageville, South Carolina

HAMBURGER SHISH KABOBS

1 lb. ground beef	1/4 c. finely chopped onion
1 egg	2 tbsp. finely chopped green
1/3 c. evaporated milk	pepper
1/2 c. fine bread crumbs	Onion slices
1 tsp. salt	Tomato slices
1/4 tsp. pepper	

Mix all ingredients except the onion and tomato slices and shape into 16 balls. Place on long skewers alternately with onion and tomato slices. Broil until brown on all sides. Serve between long pieces of split French bread, if desired. 8 servings.

Mrs. Gerald Banks, Amory, Mississippi

PINEAPPLE-BEEF BALLS

1 13 1/2-oz. can pineapple chunks	1/4 tsp. salt
2/3 c. canned beef bouillon	1/2 tsp. monosodium glutamate
2 tbsp. wine vinegar	4 tsp. cornstarch
2 tbsp. sugar	2 tbsp. cold water
1 tbsp. soy sauce	1/4 c. coarsely chopped green pepper

Drain the syrup from the pineapple and reserve syrup. Combine the reserved syrup with the bouillon, vinegar, sugar, soy sauce, salt and monosodium gluta-mate in a saucepan. Simmer for 10 minutes. Combine the cornstarch and water, then stir into the bouillon mixture and cook, stirring, until clear and thickened. Add the pineapple chunks, green pepper and Beef Balls and heat through.

Oven Beef Balls

1/2 lb. ground beef chuck	1/2 tsp. salt
1 sm. egg	1 tbsp. minced onion
1 1/2 tsp. cornstarch	Dash of pepper

Combine all ingredients and mix well. Shape into 8 balls, then place on a baking sheet. Bake at 425 degrees for 15 minutes.

Pineapple-Beef Balls (above)

PINEAPPLE-BEEF BALL BUFFET

1 13 1/2-oz. can pineapple chunks	1 lb. ground lean beef
1 c. rice	1 egg, slightly beaten
2 3/4 tsp. salt	1 c. fine soft bread crumbs
1 1-lb. can stewed tomatoes	1 tbsp. instant minced onion
1/2 tsp. dillweed	1/8 tsp. pepper
2 tbsp. chopped parsley	1/3 c. milk

Drain the pineapple and reserve syrup. Add enough water to reserved syrup to make 1 1/2 cups liquid and pour into a saucepan. Add the rice and 1 teaspoon salt and bring to a boil. Cover. Simmer for about 15 minutes or until rice is dry and fluffy. Add the pineapple, 1/2 teaspoon salt, tomatoes, dillweed and parsley. Combine remaining salt and remaining ingredients and shape into 1-inch balls. Brown on all sides in 1 tablespoon fat in a skillet. Add to pineapple mixture and mix well. Place in a 2-quart baking dish. Bake in 375-degree oven for 25 minutes or until heated through.

Mrs. Harold Pittman, Mobile, Alabama

SPICY MEATBALLS IN RED WINE SAUCE

1/2 c. chili sauce	4 slices bread, crusts removed
1 can tomato paste	3/4 c. milk
1/8 tsp. thyme	1 sm. onion, grated
1 tbsp. paprika	1 tsp. salt
1/4 c. catsup	1/2 tsp. pepper
1/8 tsp. curry powder	1 1/2 lb. ground beef
1/8 tsp. nutmeg	1 c. flour
2 c. dry red wine	5 tbsp. bacon fat
1 c. water	

Combine first 9 ingredients in a bowl and mix well. Soak the bread in milk in a mixing bowl. Add the onion, salt, pepper and beef and mix thoroughly. Shape into small meatballs and roll in flour. Cook in bacon fat in a frying pan over medium heat until golden brown, turning carefully. Remove from frying pan. Add any remaining flour to the frying pan and cook, stirring, until brown. Stir in the sauce and bring to a boil, stirring frequently. Add the meatballs and cover. Simmer for 1 hour, turning meatballs occasionally. May be frozen.

Francine Harper, Orlando, Florida

MOUSSAKA OF BEEF

1 lb. lean ground beef	2 egg whites, stiffly beaten
Salad oil	1/2 c. bread crumbs
3 med. onions, chopped	1 lge. eggplant, sliced 1/4-in. thick
1 tbsp. minced parsley	
1/3 c. water	2 tbsp. butter or margarine
1 tbsp. tomato paste	2 tbsp. flour
2 tsp. salt	1 c. milk
1/2 tsp. pepper	1 c. grated Parmesan cheese

Brown the beef in small amount of oil in a heavy skillet. Stir in the onions, parsley, water, tomato paste, salt and pepper and simmer for 25 minutes, stirring occasionally. Cool slightly. Fold in egg whites and bread crumbs. Brown the eggplant in small amount of oil in a skillet. Place alternate layers of eggplant and beef mixture in a shallow casserole. Melt the butter in a saucepan and blend in flour. Stir in the milk and cook, stirring, until thickened. Pour over casserole and sprinkle with cheese. Bake in 350-degree oven for 30 minutes or until browned. 6 servings.

Mrs. Hope Buford, Ft. Worth, Texas

GROUND BEEF-FILLED FRESH SQUASH

3 fresh acorn squash	1 tsp. salt
1 lb. ground beef	1/2 tsp. pepper
1/2 c. herb-seasoned stuffing mix	3/4 c. beef bouillon
1 tbsp. minced fresh parsley	1/2 c. sliced fresh mushrooms
2 tbsp. minced fresh onion	Butter

Cut the squash in half lengthwise and remove the seeds. Place, cut side down, in baking pan, then add 1/4 inch boiling water to pan. Bake at 350 degrees for 30 minutes or until almost tender. Saute the ground beef until crumbly. Add the stuffing mix, parsley, onion, salt, pepper and bouillon, then toss lightly to combine. Turn the squash, cut side up, then fill with the beef mixture. Return to the oven and bake for 20 to 30 minutes longer. Saute the mushrooms in butter, then arrange over stuffed squash. 6 servings.

Ground Beef-Filled Fresh Squash (above)

Meatballs and Noodles Monte Carlo (below)

MEATBALLS AND NOODLES MONTE CARLO

1 lb. ground chuck	2 No. 2 cans tomato juice
1/4 c. fine dry bread crumbs	1 env. spaghetti sauce mix
1/3 c. chopped onion	1 c. water
1 tsp. salt	1 8-oz. package noodles
Dash of pepper	1/2 c. sliced pitted ripe
2/3 c. evaporated milk	olives
1/4 c. butter	

Combine the ground chuck, bread crumbs, onion, salt, pepper and evaporated milk in a medium-sized mixing bowl and mix lightly but thoroughly. Shape mixture into 12 meatballs. Melt the butter in a large skillet over medium heat, then add the meatballs and brown evenly on all sides. Push to one side of skillet and add the tomato juice. Stir in the spaghetti sauce mix and water, blending well. Bring to a boil and stir in the noodles and olives. Cover and reduce the heat. Simmer for 15 minutes or until noodles are tender, stirring occasionally. 6 servings.

ALABAMA JOHNNY MARZETTI

1 lge. onion, chopped	1 can tomato sauce
1 green pepper, chopped	1/3 lb. Cheddar cheese, grated
1/3 c. cooking oil	1 can cream of mushroom soup
1 lb. ground beef	1 can cream-style corn
1/2 lb. ground lean pork	2 tbsp. Worcestershire sauce
1 8-oz. package egg noodles	1 can pitted ripe olives
1 can tomato soup	

Saute the onion and green pepper in the oil in a skillet until tender, then remove from skillet. Add the meats to the skillet and brown. Add the onion mixture. Cook the noodles according to package directions and add to meat mixture. Add remaining ingredients and mix well. Pour into 2 large casseroles. Cover and refrigerate overnight. Bake at 350 degrees until heated through. 12-15 servings.

Mary K. Porter, Collinsville, Alabama

SOUR CREAM-BEEF CASSEROLE

1 8-oz. package med. noodles	1 8-oz. can tomato sauce
1 lb. ground beef	1 c. cream-style cottage cheese
2 tbsp. butter	1 c. sour cream
1 tsp. salt	1/2 c. chopped green onions
1/8 tsp. pepper	3/4 c. shredded sharp Cheddar
1/4 tsp. garlic salt	cheese

Cook the noodles according to package directions. Brown the beef in butter in a skillet. Add salt, pepper, garlic salt and tomato sauce and simmer for 5 minutes. Combine the cottage cheese, sour cream, onions and noodles. Place alternate layers of noodle mixture and beef mixture in a casserole and top with Cheddar cheese. Bake at 350 degrees for 25 to 30 minutes. 10-12 servings.

Rhonda Alexander, Perry, Florida

LASAGNA-SPINACH CASSEROLE

1/2 c. chopped onion	2 3-oz. cans sliced mushrooms
1 garlic clove, chopped	1 8-oz. package lasagna
2 lb. ground beef	2 eggs, slightly beaten
2 tbsp. salad oil	1 pkg. frozen chopped spinach
2 tsp. salt	1 c. grated Parmesan cheese
4 8-oz. cans tomato sauce	1/2 pt. small curd cottage
1 6-oz. can tomato paste	cheese
1 tsp. oregano	1 pkg. sliced American cheese

Brown the onion, garlic and ground beef in 1 tablespoon salad oil in a skillet and season with 1 teaspoon salt. Combine the tomato sauce, tomato paste, oregano and mushrooms in a saucepan and simmer for 15 minutes. Cook the lasagna according to package directions and drain. Cool slightly and mix with 1 egg. Cook the spinach according to package directions and drain. Mix with Parmesan cheese and remaining egg, oil and salt. Pour half the tomato mixture into a 15 x 10 x 2-inch baking pan and cover with half the lasagna. Add spinach mixture and cottage cheese and cover with remaining lasagna. Add the beef mixture and cover with remaining tomato mixture. Cover with foil. Bake at 350 degrees for 55 minutes. Remove foil and cover with American cheese. Bake until cheese is melted. Cut in squares to serve. 6 servings.

Nancy Andrews, Austin, Texas

BEEF D' AMANDE CASSEROLE

1 lb. ground beef	1 can cream of mushroom soup
1 c. diced celery	1 can cream of celery soup
1/2 c. diced onion	2 c. milk
1/4 c. diced green pepper	2 c. cooked noodles
1 tsp. seasoned salt	1/4 c. slivered almonds
1/8 tsp. seasoned pepper	1 c. crushed potato chips
1/8 tsp. crushed basil leaves	

Saute the beef, celery, onion and green pepper in a skillet for about 10 minutes, then pour off grease. Add the seasonings, soups and milk and mix thoroughly. Stir in the noodles and almonds and place in a greased 2-quart casserole. Cover. Bake for 30 minutes at 350 degrees. Uncover and sprinkle with potato chips. Bake for 15 minutes longer. 6-8 servings.

Mrs. Kerry Dowell, Albuquerque, New Mexico

PASTITSIO

1 lge. onion, chopped fine	Salt and pepper to taste
6 tbsp. butter	1/2 c. white wine
2 lb. ground beef	1 lb. elbow macaroni
1/2 can tomato paste	1 lb. grated Parmesan cheese
1/2 c. water	2 eggs, well beaten
1/2 tsp. ground cinnamon	1 c. milk
1/2 tsp. ground nutmeg	

Saute the onion in 2 tablespoons butter in a skillet. Add the beef and cook, stirring, until brown. Add the tomato paste, water, spices, seasonings and wine and simmer until thickened. Cook the macaroni in boiling, salted water until tender, then drain. Melt remaining butter and pour over macaroni, mixing carefully. Spread half the macaroni in a 9 x 13-inch pan and sprinkle with half the cheese. Spread beef sauce over macaroni and cover with remaining macaroni. Top with remaining cheese. Mix the eggs and milk and pour over cheese. Bake at 350 degrees for 45 minutes. Cool slightly and cut in squares. 12 servings.

Mrs. George Dowqwillo, Montgomery, Alabama

MOCK RAVIOLI

1 1/2 lb. ground beef	1 tsp. oregano
3 onions, finely chopped	1 tsp. sage
1 garlic clove, finely chopped	1/2 c. chopped parsley
Salt and pepper to taste	1 can sliced mushrooms
1 lb. shell or bow macaroni	2 cans tomato sauce
1 No. 2 can spinach	1 c. diced cheese
1 tsp. rosemary	

Brown the beef, onions, garlic, salt and pepper in a skillet. Cook the macaroni according to package directions. Combine the spinach, herbs, parsley, mushrooms and tomato sauce in a saucepan and cook for 30 minutes. Place alternate layers of beef mixture, macaroni and spinach mixture in a greased casserole and top with cheese. Bake at 350 degrees for about 30 minutes. One package frozen chopped spinach may be substituted for canned spinach. 6-8 servings.

Mrs. C. F. Finklea, Phoenix, Arizona

MINI LOAVES STROGANOFF ON FLUFFY RICE

1 lb. ground beef	1 c. soft bread crumbs
1 1 7/8-oz. envelope	2 tbsp. catsup
stroganoff sauce mix	3/4 c. milk
1 egg, lightly beaten	4 servings cooked rice

Combine the ground beef with 2 tablespoons of the sauce mix, then add the egg, bread crumbs and catsup and mix well. Press the beef mixture into four 6-ounce custard cups, then turn out onto a shallow baking pan. Bake in a 325-degree oven for 25 minutes. Blend the remaining sauce mix with the milk in a small saucepan and cook until thickened, stirring constantly. Cover and keep hot. Arrange the rice evenly on serving platter. Transfer baked loaves onto rice and spoon a small amount of the sauce over the loaves and rice. Serve remaining sauce in gravy boat. Garnish loaves with chopped parsley. 4 servings.

Mini Loaves Stroganoff on Fluffy Rice (above)

163

Chili Croquettes (below)

CHILI CROQUETTES

4 c. cooked ground beef	1/4 tsp. pepper
2 c. thick white sauce	1/4 tsp. garlic powder
1 c. bread crumbs	Flour
2 tbsp. instant minced onions	1 egg, lightly beaten
2 1/2 tsp. salt	1 tbsp. milk or water
4 tsp. chili powder	Bread crumbs

Combine the first 8 ingredients and mix well. Shape into pyramids and chill thoroughly. Roll in flour. Combine the egg and milk, then dip pyramids in the egg mixture and roll in crumbs. Fry in hot deep fat for 2 minutes or until browned. Serve with tomato sauce. 6 servings.

BEEF PATTIES WITH WINE SAUCE

1 1/2 lb. ground beef	1/2 c. beef broth
1/2 c. heavy cream	2/3 c. dry red wine
2 tbsp. chopped onions	1/2 lb. sliced mushrooms,
1 1/2 tsp. salt	sauteed
1/2 tsp. freshly ground pepper	6 slices French bread, sauteed
3 tbsp. butter	3 tbsp. chopped parsley
1 tbsp. cornstarch	

Mix the beef, cream, onions, salt and pepper and shape into 6 thick patties. Melt the butter in a skillet. Add the patties and cook to desired doneness, turning once. Remove from skillet and keep warm. Mix the cornstarch with broth and add to the skillet. Add the wine and bring to boiling point. Add the patties and mushrooms and cook over low heat for 3 minutes. Place a patty on each piece of bread and pour sauce over patties. Sprinkle with parsley. 6 servings.

Mrs. Glenda Luke Mitchell, Weatherford, Texas

GRILLED HAMBURGERS

1 1/2 lb. ground lean beef	1/4 c. melted butter or oil
4 cheese slices	1/4 c. sherry
4 bacon slices	Salt and pepper to taste
1/4 c. soy sauce	

Shape beef into 8 thin patties and place 1 slice of cheese between 2 patties. Wrap bacon slice around edge and fasten with toothpick. Combine the soy sauce, butter and sherry, then brush on the patties. Broil over hot coals until done, turning once. Sprinkle with salt and pepper. Serve hot. 4 servings.

Flacie Patterson, Terral, Oklahoma

HAMBURGER STEAKS WITH PANCHO SAUCE

1 med. onion, chopped	1/4 tsp. pepper
2 cloves of garlic, minced	1/4 c. crumbled Roquefort
3 tbsp. salad oil	cheese
2 lb. ground beef chuck	2 tbsp. soft butter
2 eggs, beaten	2 tbsp. brandy
1 tbsp. chopped parsley	Salad oil
1 tsp. salt	

Saute the onion and garlic in oil in a skillet until onion is tender. Cool. Add the beef, eggs, parsley, salt and pepper and mix well. Shape into 4 balls. Blend the cheese, butter and brandy in a bowl. Make a deep hole in each ball and place 1/4 of the cheese mixture in each hole. Shape beef mixture over cheese mixture to form patties. Brush with oil and sprinkle with additional salt and pepper. Place on a broiler pan. Broil about 5 inches from heat for about 15 minutes for medium-doneness, turning once.

Pancho Sauce

1 c. catsup	1/4 tsp. salt
1/2 c. mayonnaise	2 tbsp. pineapple juice
1/2 c. chili sauce	1 tbsp. wine vinegar
1 tbsp. dry mustard	2 tsp. Worcestershire sauce
1 tsp. prepared horseradish	3 drops of hot sauce
1/2 tsp. ground ginger	

Combine all ingredients in a bowl and serve with steaks. May be heated, if desired.

Mrs. H. M. Hightower, Winston-Salem, North Carolina

Saucy Ground Beef Fillets (below)

SAUCY GROUND BEEF FILLETS

2 lb. ground chuck	1/3 c. milk
3 tbsp. chopped onion	1 pkg. complete spaghetti
3/4 c. bread crumbs	sauce mix
1/4 tsp. salt	8 bacon strips
1 egg	

Preheat oven to 375 degrees. Combine the chuck, onion, crumbs, salt, egg and milk and mix together with a fork. Shape into 8 patties. Place the spaghetti sauce mix on waxed paper, then coat all sides of each patty heavily with the mix. Wrap bacon around each patty and secure with toothpick, then place in a baking pan. Bake for 30 minutes.

MUSHROOMS STUFFED WITH HAMBURGER

Large mushrooms	1/4 c. cold water
Salt and pepper to taste	1/2 tsp. lemon juice
1 lb. ground round steak	1 onion, grated
1 tbsp. fine bread crumbs	1 tsp. thick steak sauce
1 egg	Bacon slices, cut in half

Cut stems from mushrooms, leaving cavity. Grind the stems and reserve. Wash the mushroom caps and drain. Sprinkle with salt and pepper. Combine the ground steak, crumbs, egg, water, lemon juice, onion, steak sauce and reserved mushroom stems and fill mushroom caps, rounding tops. Place in a buttered pan and place bacon over top. Bake at 350 degrees for 15 minutes.

Deborah Wiggins, Columbia, South Carolina

BEEF-STUFFED PEPPERS

8 green peppers	4 med. tomatoes
1 sm. onion, chopped	1 1/2 c. cut fresh corn
1 lb. ground beef	Salt and pepper to taste
2 tbsp. fat	Buttered bread crumbs

Remove tops and seeds from green peppers. Cook in boiling water for 5 minutes and drain. Brown the onion and beef in hot fat in a skillet. Add the tomatoes, corn and seasonings. Stuff the green peppers with beef mixture and top with crumbs. Stand upright in a greased baking dish and add a small amount of water. Cover. Bake at 350 degrees for 1 hour.

Betty Rooks, Bethlehem, Georgia

BEEF-STUFFED GREEN PEPPERS

3 green peppers	1 egg, beaten
1 tsp. salt	Catsup
1/8 tsp. pepper	1/4 c. finely chopped onion
1 tbsp. Worcestershire sauce	1 1/2 lb. ground beef
1/3 c. oats	

Cut the green peppers in half lengthwise and remove the seeds. Cook in boiling, salted water for 5 minutes, then invert and drain thoroughly. Combine the salt, pepper, Worcestershire sauce, oats, egg, 1/3 cup catsup, onion and ground beef and mix thoroughly. Pack about 1/2 cup of the beef mixture into each green pepper half, then place the peppers in a 12 x 8-inch baking dish. Top each stuffed pepper with 2 teaspoons catsup. Bake at 350 degrees for 30 to 35 minutes. 6 servings.

RICE-STUFFED PEPPERS

3 lge. green peppers	2 8-oz. cans tomato sauce
3 tbsp. minced onion	1/2 c. sherry
2 tbsp. butter	1 c. sour cream
1 lb. ground beef	1/4 lb. sharp Cheddar cheese,
1 c. cooked rice	grated
1/2 tsp. salt	

Cut the green peppers into halves lengthwise and remove seeds and stems. Place in a large saucepan of boiling, salted water and remove from heat. Let stand for 5 minutes. Drain and arrange in a baking dish. Saute the onion in butter for 5 minutes. Add the ground beef, rice, salt and 1 can tomato sauce and place in green peppers. Combine remaining tomato sauce, 1/2 cup water, sherry and sour cream and pour over stuffed peppers. Bake at 350 degrees for 40 minutes. Sprinkle with cheese and bake for 20 minutes longer.

Mrs. Louise Freeman, Jackson, Mississippi

Stuffed Peppers (below)

STUFFED PEPPERS

1 3/4-oz. envelope brown	1 tbsp. instant minced onion
gravy mix	1 tsp. salt
1 c. tomato juice	1/4 tsp. pepper
1 lb. ground beef	4 or 5 green peppers
1 egg	

Place the gravy mix in a small saucepan, then stir in the tomato juice. Bring just to a boil, stirring constantly. Combine the remaining ingredients except the peppers, then add 1/4 cup of the prepared gravy and mix well. Remove the tops and seeds from peppers, and fill with the beef mixture. Place in a shallow baking dish and cover. Bake in a 375-degree oven for 45 to 50 minutes or until tender. Transfer peppers to serving dish. Heat the remaining gravy and pour over the peppers. 4-5 servings.

STUFFED TOMATOES

6 to 8 tomatoes	1 tsp. dried mint
1 lb. ground chuck	1 tsp. salt
1/2 c. chopped onion	1/2 c. rice
1 No. 2 can tomatoes	1 tbsp. brown sugar
1 tsp. parsley flakes	

Cut the tops from tomatoes and reserve. Remove pulp from tomatoes. Invert tomato shells to drain. Brown the beef and onion in a skillet. Add remaining ingredients and bring to a boil. Fill tomatoes with beef mixture and replace reserved tops. Place in a baking dish. Bake at 350 degrees for 1 hour or until rice is tender.

Cleo Codas, Durham, North Carolina

BRUNSWICK STEW

1 lb. sliced salt pork	3 1/2 qt. lima beans
1 5-lb. hen	3 to 6 lge. onions, chopped
2 lb. ground beef	1/2 gal. diced potatoes
1 peck tomatoes, peeled	1 1/2 doz. ears of corn, cut from cob
2 hot green peppers	Salt to taste
1 lge. head cabbage, chopped	

Fry the salt pork in a large kettle until brown. Add remaining ingredients and bring to a boil. Reduce heat and cover. Simmer for about 4 hours, stirring occasionally as mixture begins to thicken and adding water, if needed. Remove chicken and cool. Remove chicken from bones and add to the stew. Heat through. 50 servings.

Ialeen S. Mode, Franklinton, North Carolina

CAMP STEW FOR TWO HUNDRED

10 cooked hens with broth	12 qt. lima beans
15 lb. ground beef	10 qt. corn
20 lb. ground pork	10 gal. tomatoes
6 gal. chopped potatoes	2 1/2 lb. butter
8 qt. chopped onions	Hot sauce to taste
10 qt. peas	Salt and pepper to taste

Remove chicken from bones and chop the meat into small pieces. Cook the beef and pork in a large pot until lightly browned. Add the chicken, broth and remaining ingredients and cook for 4 hours, stirring very frequently.

Mrs. Clarence M. Williams, Liberty, North Carolina

BARBECUED HAMBURGER FOR A CROWD OF FIFTY

5 lb. ground beef	1 c. brown sugar
5 green peppers, chopped	1 c. mustard
5 onions, chopped	1/2 c. Worcestershire sauce
2 c. chopped celery	2 1/2 tsp. chili powder
2 bottles catsup	Salt and pepper to taste

Brown the beef, green peppers, onions and celery in a large kettle, then add the remaining ingredients. Simmer for 1 hour. Serve on split buns.

Mrs. Marion Fuechsel, New Orleans, Louisiana

BEEF AND VEGETABLE-FILLED BUNS FOR TWENTY-FIVE

1/2 lb. cabbage, coarsely ground	1/2 lb. onions, coarsely ground
1/2 lb. potatoes, coarsely ground	Salt to taste
3 c. ground fresh tomatoes	1 1/2 lb. ground beef
1/2 lb. carrots, coarsely ground	1 c. prepared mustard
	1 c. finely chopped tomatoes
	1 sm. onion, chopped
	Heated hamburger buns

Season the ground vegetables with salt, then season the beef and fold into the ground vegetable mixture. Place in a greased, shallow pan. Bake at 350 degrees for 1 hour. Combine the mustard, chopped tomatoes and chopped onion and heat through. Split the buns and cover the bottom halves with beef mixture, then spread the mustard mixture on top halves. Place halves together and serve immediately.

Willia Mae Cornwell, Waco, Texas

CALIFORNIA TAMALE PIE FOR TWENTY

3 lb. ground beef	1 can chopped ripe olives
1 lge. onion, ground	24 tortillas
1 green pepper, ground	1/2 lb. Cheddar cheese, grated
1 block chili	2 8-oz. cans tomato sauce
1 No. 303 can kidney beans	2 sauce cans water

Brown the beef, then add the onion, green pepper and chili. Simmer until the chili is melted. Add the beans and olives and mix well. Place 1 tablespoon of the beef mixture in each tortilla and roll up. Place 1 layer of filled tortillas, seam side down, in large baking pan. Sprinkle with cheese. Repeat layers until all tortillas are used. Pour any remaining beef mixture over and around rolls. Pour the tomato sauce and water over top and cover. Bake for 1 hour and 30 minutes at 300 degrees.

Mrs. Richard Tuck, Bethesda, Maryland

CHINESE HASH FOR ONE HUNDRED

15 lb. ground beef	2 qt. diced celery
8 c. rice	2 50-oz. cans mushroom soup
8 qt. water	2 c. soy sauce
1/2 c. chicken soup base	1 No. 10 can bean sprouts
1 c. dried minced onions	

Brown the ground beef in large kettle, then drain off fat. Cook the rice in water and soup base until tender. Add the onions, celery, soup, soy sauce and bean sprouts to the beef and simmer for about 10 minutes. Combine the rice with the beef mixture, then heat and serve.

Mrs. Doris Styker, Miami, Florida

ENCHILADA CASSEROLE FOR THIRTY

5 lb. ground beef	30 corn tortillas
5 med. onions, chopped	5 4 1/2-oz. jars chopped
10 cans tomato paste	olives
Salt and pepper to taste	2 lb. sharp Cheddar cheese,
Chili powder to taste	grated
10 c. water	

Saute the beef and onions until lightly browned, then add tomato paste. Season with salt, pepper and chili powder, then stir in the water. Simmer the sauce until well blended. Arrange alternate layers of tortillas, beef sauce, olives and cheese in casserole. Bake in a 350-degree oven for about 30 minutes.

Mrs. Margaret Whiteside, Yuma, Arizona

HAMBURGER-MACARONI FOR TWENTY-FIVE

2 lb. macaroni	1 tsp. seasoning salt
3 lb. ground beef	1 tsp. onion salt
4 No. 303 cans tomatoes	4 cans Cheddar cheese soup
1 tsp. salt	

Cook the macaroni according to package directions and drain. Saute the ground beef until lightly browned, then add the macaroni, tomatoes and seasonings and mix well. Cover with the soup and simmer for 1 hour.

Ruby Dotson, Enid, Oklahoma

LASAGNA FOR FIFTY

5 lb. ground beef	1 tbsp. salt
1 No. 10 can tomato puree	3 c. water
4 c. catsup	5 lb. lasagna
1/2 lb. onions, chopped	5 lb. cottage cheese
1 clove of garlic, minced	2 doz. eggs, beaten
2 tbsp. Worcestershire sauce	4 lb. mozzarella cheese, sliced
1 tsp. cayenne pepper	1 1/2 c. grated Parmesan cheese

Saute the ground beef until lightly browned, then add the puree, catsup, onions, garlic, Worcestershire sauce, cayenne pepper, salt and water. Simmer for 15 minutes. Cook the lasagna according to package directions, then rinse and drain. Combine the cottage cheese and eggs. Place a layer of beef sauce in bottom of two 12 x 18 x 2 1/2-inch pans, then add a layer of noodles and another layer of beef sauce. Spread a layer of egg mixture over the beef mixture, then top with mozzarella cheese and sprinkle with Parmesan. Repeat layers until all ingredients are used, ending with beef sauce and Parmesan cheese. Bake at 375 degrees for 40 minutes.

Mrs. Betty King, Chattanooga, Tennessee

TOMATO SAUCE MEAT LOAF FOR TWENTY-FIVE

1 1-lb. 12-oz. can tomatoes, mashed	1/2 c. chopped onion
4 c. soft bread crumbs	1/2 c. chopped parsley
4 lb. ground beef	8 slices bacon, cut in half
2 lb. ground pork	4 cans tomato soup
3 env. French salad dressing mix	1/4 c. prepared horseradish
4 eggs	1/4 c. prepared mustard
2 c. chopped celery	1/4 tsp. cloves
	1/8 tsp. pepper

Combine the tomatoes and bread crumbs and set aside. Combine the beef, pork, salad dressing mix, eggs, celery, onion and parsley and mix well, then stir in the tomato mixture. Shape into 2 loaves and place in a shallow baking pan. Place bacon strips crosswise over tops of loaves. Bake at 375 degrees for 45 to 50 minutes. Combine the remaining ingredients in a saucepan and heat thoroughly, stirring frequently. Pour over meat loaves when ready to serve.

Mrs. Angie Murrey, St. Petersburg, Florida

BEEF AND POTATO CASSEROLE FOR TWENTY-FIVE

3/4 c. margarine	1/2 lb. onions, chopped
3/4 c. flour	1 tbsp. lemon juice
2 qt. milk	1/2 tsp. mustard
Salt	1 1/2 tsp. Worcestershire sauce
3 lb. ground beef	10 lb. potatoes, diced
1 lb. sausage	1/2 lb. cheese, grated

Melt the margarine in a large saucepan, then stir in the flour until smooth. Add the milk gradually and cook over low heat, stirring, until thickened. Season with salt to taste. Brown the beef, sausage and onions, then add 2 tablespoons salt, lemon juice, mustard and Worcestershire sauce. Mix the beef mixture with the white sauce and pour over the potatoes. Stir in the cheese and mix well. Place in baking dishes. Bake at 325 degrees until potatoes are tender.

Mamie L. Winfrey, West Fork, Arkansas

DELICIOUS BEEF-CHEDDAR CASSEROLE FOR TWENTY

1 lb. egg noodles	1 lge. can whole kernel corn, drained
1 c. chopped onion	2 tbsp. chili powder
2 tbsp. butter or margarine	Salt to taste
4 lb. ground beef chuck	1 lb. Cheddar cheese, grated
1 1/2 c. chopped green peppers	
6 8-oz. cans tomato sauce	

Cook the noodles according to package directions and drain. Saute the onion in butter in large skillet until soft, then add the beef and cook until browned, stirring to break up large pieces. Add the peppers, tomato sauce, corn, chili powder and salt and mix well. Combine the beef mixture with the noodles, then place into 3 greased baking dishes. Top with cheese. Bake at 350 degrees for 1 hour.

Mrs. Laura Clark, Arlington, Virginia

PARTY PIZZA QUICKIES FOR TWENTY-FOUR

3 c. tomato paste	1/2 lb. butter
1 tsp. garlic salt	2 lb. ground beef
3/4 tsp. onion salt	2 doz. buns
2 tbsp. oregano	1 1/2 lb. shredded American or
2 tbsp. parsley flakes	Cheddar cheese

Combine the tomato paste, garlic and onion salts, oregano, parsley flakes and butter. Cook for 35 minutes over medium heat, stirring frequently. Brown the ground beef lightly and combine with the sauce. Cool. Spread on the sliced buns, then sprinkle with cheese. Place on a cookie sheet. Bake in 400-degree oven for about 8 minutes or until cheese is melted and bubbly.

Mrs. Polly Burns, Knoxville, Tennessee

MARQUIS STEAKS FOR ONE HUNDRED

5 lb. cottage cheese	1 1/2 lb. bread crumbs
4 c. milk	4 tbsp. salt
1/2 lb. onions, chopped	12 lb. ground beef

Combine all the ingredients except the beef and blend well. Add the beef and mix well. Shape into patties and place in baking pans. Bake for 25 minutes in 350-degree oven. Thicken the drippings for gravy and pour over patties.

Mrs. Melba Coleman, Gainesville, Georgia

SLOPPY JOES FOR ONE HUNDRED

35 lb. hamburger	2 c. celery seed
18 c. catsup	1/2 c. salt
9 c. chili sauce	2 tbsp. pepper
1 c. sugar	20 med. onions, finely chopped
2 c. prepared mustard	5 bunches celery, finely
3 lge. peppers, finely chopped	chopped
2 c. vinegar	

Place the hamburger in a large canner on medium heat. Cook, stirring constantly, until crumbly. Add the remaining ingredients and cook slowly, stirring frequently, for about 3 hours. Serve between buns.

Mrs. Doris Jackson, Prescott, Arizona

SPAGHETTI AND MEATBALLS FOR FIFTY

10 lb. ground beef	4 1/2 qt. canned tomatoes
6 c. fine dry bread crumbs	5 c. tomato sauce
5 tsp. garlic salt	3 cloves of garlic, minced
12 eggs	1 1/4 c. finely chopped onions
Salt	2 1/2 tsp. oregano
2 1/2 tsp. pepper	5 lb. spaghetti
1 1/4 c. olive or salad oil	7 1/2 gal. boiling water

Combine the beef, bread crumbs, garlic salt, eggs, 5 teaspoons salt and 1 1/4 teaspoons pepper and mix well. Shape into 1-inch balls. Cook in oil until lightly browned on all sides. Place tomatoes, tomato sauce, garlic, onions, 2 tablespoons salt, pepper and oregano in large kettle. Cover and cook over low heat for 1 hour, stirring occasionally, then add the meatballs. Simmer for 30 minutes. Add the spaghetti to rapidly boiling water, then cover and cook until tender, stirring occasionally. Drain. Serve meatballs and sauce over spaghetti.

Mrs. Nancy Mims, Hammond, Louisiana

SWEDISH HAMBURGER STEAK FOR FORTY

15 lb. finely ground hamburger	1 clove of garlic, pressed
3 tbsp. salt	6 eggs, slightly beaten
2 tsp. pepper	Cooking oil
1 sm. loaf bread, cubed	1 c. (scant) flour
4 med. onions, grated	1 box onion soup mix
1 lge. can evaporated milk	2 cans consomme

Combine the hamburger, salt, pepper, bread, onions, milk, 1 milk can water, garlic and eggs and mix well. Shape into patties and brown in small amount of oil. Place in large pans. Combine the flour and soup mix in a large saucepan, then stir in the consomme gradually until well blended. Add 2 consomme cans water and cook, stirring constantly, until thickened. Pour over patties and simmer for 1 hour, adding water if needed.

Mrs. Emory C. Gilbert, Montezuma, Georgia

SWEDISH MEATBALLS IN BURGUNDY FOR TWENTY

3 lb. ground beef chuck	1/2 c. salad oil
3 c. fine dry bread crumbs	1 c. flour
4 sm. onions, minced	1 1/2 qt. water
3 tsp. cornstarch	3 3/4 c. Burgundy
1/4 tsp. allspice	8 beef bouillon cubes
4 beaten eggs	1 tsp. pepper
3 c. light cream	1 tsp. sugar
4 tsp. salt	Bottled gravy sauce

Combine the beef, crumbs, onions, cornstarch, allspice, eggs, cream and 3 teaspoons salt and mix well. Shape into 90 to 100 balls. Drop the balls, several at a time, into hot oil in a Dutch oven. Brown well, then transfer to plate. Stir the flour into the drippings, then add the water, Burgundy, bouillon cubes, remaining salt, pepper, sugar and enough gravy sauce to tint light brown. Cook, stirring until smooth, then arrange the meatballs in the sauce. Simmer, covered, for 30 minutes. Serve in a 4-quart chafing dish, if desired. May be made a day in advance and reheated.

Mrs. Patsy Miller, Norfolk, Virginia

CHILI FOR A CROWD OF SIXTEEN

1 lb. dry pinto beans	6 lb. ground chuck
2 qt. water	1/2 c. minced parsley
2 14 1/2-oz. cans tomato puree	2/3 c. chili powder
7 c. tomatoes	2 tbsp. salt
4 c. chopped onions	2 tsp. pepper
4 c. chopped green peppers	2 tsp. cumin
1/4 c. oil	2 tsp. monosodium glutamate

Place the beans in the water in a large kettle. Cover and bring to a boil, then boil for 5 minutes. Remove from heat. Let stand in tightly covered pan for 1 hour, then bring to a boil. Reduce heat and simmer, covered, for 1 hour and 30 minutes. Add the puree and tomatoes and simmer for 5 minutes longer. Saute the onions and green peppers in oil, then drain off excess fat. Add the ground chuck and remaining ingredients and simmer for 10 minutes. Combine with the beans. Cover and simmer for 45 minutes. Uncover and simmer for 30 minutes longer. Remove any excess fat. Serve hot in bowls with crisp corn chips.

Barbara Harper, Huntington, Texas

SALISBURY STEAK WITH SAUCE FOR TWENTY

5 lb. hamburger	5 eggs
1 onion, finely chopped	2 1/2 c. milk
2 stalks celery, chopped	Salt and pepper to taste
1 1/4 c. rolled oats	1 green pepper, minced

Combine all ingredients and mix well, then shape into 20 patties. Brown on both sides and place in a roaster.

Steak Sauce

2 c. (packed) brown sugar	1 tsp. chili powder
4 tbsp. prepared mustard	1/2 gal. tomato puree

Combine the brown sugar, mustard and chili powder, then add the tomato puree and blend well. Pour over the patties. Bake in a 325-degree oven for 30 to 45 minutes.

Mrs. Caroline Nixon, Tuscaloosa, Alabama

175

Picadillo (page 181)

sauces

Nothing peps up ground beef like a complementary sauce. Knowing this, *Southern Living* readers — women who have spent years learning about the foods their families love best — have created exciting, zesty sauces for every kind of ground beef dish.

Serving chopped steak? Then give it an easy gourmet touch with No-cook Bernaise Sauce. This simplified version of the great French sauce will add so much to your chopped steak dish.

Or top that meat loaf with Savory Barbecue Sauce . . . its bite will make even the dullest appetite come wide awake! Mustard Sauce is another natural for meat loaves, too.

And don't forget the sauce for spaghetti. Serve Italian Spaghetti Sauce to your hungry family and listen to the compliments flow! Spaghetti sauce . . . meat loaf sauce . . . steak sauce . . . these and more are the home-tested sauces southern cooks share with you in this recipe-filled section.

Won't it be nice to know that the sauce or gravy you're preparing to top that great main dish will be just perfect? You can cook with confidence using the recipes in this section . . . in fact, why not plan to serve ground beef and sauce tonight. You'll be so glad you did!

NINETEENTH HOLE BARBECUE SAUCE

2 tbsp. instant minced onion	1/2 tsp. cloves
1 tbsp. brown sugar	1 bay leaf
1 tbsp. mustard seed	1 clove of garlic, minced
1 tsp. monosodium glutamate	1 c. catsup
2 tsp. paprika	1/2 c. water
1 tsp. oregano	1/4 c. olive or salad oil
1 tsp. chili powder	1/4 c. tarragon vinegar
1 tsp. pepper	2 tbsp. Worcestershire sauce
1/2 tsp. salt	2 or 3 drops of liquid smoke

Combine all ingredients in a saucepan and stir well. Simmer for 20 to 25 minutes. Remove bay leaf. Serve over beef. 2 cups.

Mrs. Ginger Crowe, Huntsville, Alabama

SAVORY BARBECUE SAUCE

2 tbsp. vegetable oil	1 tsp. salt
1/2 c. chopped onions	1 tsp. pepper
1 c. catsup	2 tsp. chili powder
1/4 c. vinegar	1/2 tsp. paprika
2 tbsp. Worcestershire sauce	1 c. water

Combine all ingredients in a bowl. Brush on hamburgers, spareribs or chicken during last 30 minutes of cooking.

Mrs. Vincent Kelly, El Paso, Texas

WINE BARBECUE SAUCE

1 med. onion, chopped	1/2 tsp. pepper
4 tbsp. olive oil	2 tbsp. salt
1 clove of garlic, minced	3 tsp. brown sugar
1/2 c. finely chopped celery	2 tbsp. lemon juice
2 tbsp. Worcestershire sauce	3/4 c. catsup
2 tbsp. wine vinegar	Dash of hot sauce
1 tsp. horseradish	1/2 c. water
1 tsp. prepared mustard	1/2 c. red wine

Combine all ingredients except wine in a saucepan and simmer for 20 minutes. Add the wine and simmer for 10 minutes longer.

Mrs. F. T. Merchant, Lawton, Oklahoma

DOUBLE CHILI SAUCE

2 lb. ground beef	3 cloves of garlic, minced
1 lge. onion, chopped	Shortening

1 can chili beans	**1/2 bottle catsup**
1 can tomato sauce	**1/2 tsp. vinegar**
1 can tomatoes	**1 tbsp. mustard**
1 bell pepper, chopped	**1 sm. bottle chili powder**
1/2 tsp. hot sauce	**3 tbsp. instant flour**

Brown the beef, onion and garlic in small amount of shortening in a kettle. Add remaining ingredients and cook over low heat for 1 hour, stirring frequently. May be served with hamburgers, hot dogs or spaghetti.

Mrs. C. J. Lamberth, Byromville, Georgia

CHUCK WAGON CHILI SAUCE

1 sm. can green chili peppers	**1/2 c. vinegar**
1 lge. can tomatoes, chopped	**1/2 c. sugar**
1 env. onion soup mix	**1/2 tsp. salt**

Drain the green chili peppers, then peel and chop. Place in a saucepan. Add remaining ingredients and simmer until thickened. 10-12 servings.

Mrs. Al Hunter, Columbia, South Carolina

OLIVE SAUCE FOR TOSTADAS

1 or 2 canned green chilies, seeded	**1/4 c. sliced scallions or green onions**
4 med. peeled tomatoes, chopped	**1 tsp. salt**
	1 c. sliced pimento-stuffed olives

Blend the chilies, tomatoes, scallions and salt in electric blender until smooth. Add the olives and serve with tortillas.

Olive Sauce for Tostadas (above)

FAR EASTERN CURRY SAUCE

1/4 c. butter or margarine	1 tsp. salt
1/3 c. finely chopped onion	1/4 tsp. ginger
1/4 c. flour	1/8 tsp. pepper
4 tsp. curry powder	2 c. milk
2 tsp. sugar	2 tsp. lemon juice

Melt the butter in a medium saucepan over low heat. Add the onion and saute for about 5 minutes or until golden. Remove from heat. Add the flour, curry powder, sugar, salt, ginger and pepper and stir until smooth. Add the milk and cook over medium heat, stirring constantly, until mixture comes to a boil. Reduce heat and simmer for 1 minute. Stir in the lemon juice. 2 1/2 cups.

Helen White, Parkersburg, Virginia

DILL SAUCE

2 tbsp. butter	1 egg yolk, beaten
2 tbsp. flour	1/4 tsp. salt
1 c. evaporated milk	Dash of pepper
1/3 c. water	1 tsp. dillseed

Melt the butter in a small saucepan. Remove from heat and blend in flour. Stir in the milk and water slowly and cook over low heat, stirring constantly, until mixture comes to a boil. Stir small amount of sauce into egg yolk, then stir back into remaining hot sauce. Cook until mixture comes to boil, stirring constantly. Remove from heat and season with salt, pepper and dillseed. 1 1/2 cups.

Mrs. D. D. Wilson, Rockville, Maryland

BEST BEEF GRAVY

1/4 c. beef drippings	1/8 tsp. pepper
1/4 c. flour	2 c. beef stock or bouillon
1 tsp. salt	1 tsp. meat extract paste

Mix the beef drippings, flour, salt, and pepper in a saucepan until smooth. Cook over low heat, stirring, for about 5 minutes or until flour is lightly browned. Add the beef stock gradually and bring to boiling point, stirring constantly. Reduce heat and add the meat extract paste. Stir until paste is dissolved, then simmer for 1 minute longer. 2 cups.

Donna English, New Castle, Delaware

BEEF-TOMATO GRAVY

2 tbsp. shortening	Salt and pepper to taste
1 lb. ground beef	1/4 c. chopped onion (opt.)
1 can tomatoes	1/4 c. diced green
1 c. water	peppers (opt.)

Melt the shortening in a saucepan over medium heat. Add the ground beef and cook until brown. Add the tomatoes and water and season with salt and pepper. Add the onion and green peppers and cook over medium heat for about 1 hour, stirring occasionally.

Christine Angelloz, Rosedale, Louisiana

GROUND BEEF GRAVY

1 c. ground beef	Salt and pepper to taste
1 onion, diced	1 tbsp. flour

Brown the beef and onion in a small amount of fat in a skillet and add the salt, pepper and 1 cup water. Cook for about 10 minutes. Mix the flour with 1 tablespoon water and stir into the beef mixture. Cook, stirring, until thickened.

Mrs. Louise Liles, Covington, Kentucky

WINE-MUSHROOM GRAVY

1 tbsp. butter or margarine	2 tbsp. pimento strips
1/4 c. thinly sliced onion	1 can cream of mushroom soup
1 tbsp. chopped green pepper	1/3 c. dry white wine

Melt the butter in a medium skillet over low heat. Add the onion and green pepper and saute until tender. Remove from heat. Add the pimento strips, undiluted soup and wine and mix well. Simmer for 5 minutes, stirring occasionally. 1 1/2 cups.

Natalie Deramus, Memphis, Tennessee

PICADILLO

1/2 c. raisins	1 tbsp. vinegar
1 sm. onion, diced	1 tsp. sugar
1 clove of garlic	1 tsp. salt
1/4 c. green pepper, diced	2 bay leaves
1 lb. lean chopped beef	1/4 tsp. oregano
3 tbsp. oil	1 tbsp. angostura aromatic
1 c. canned tomatoes	bitters
1 8-oz. can tomato sauce	1/4 c. sliced olives

Combine the raisins and 1/4 cup hot water and let stand for 15 minutes. Saute the onion, garlic, green pepper and beef in oil, stirring until beef is browned. Remove the garlic, then add the remaining ingredients. Cover and simmer for 20 minutes. Garnish with whole pimento and serve with rice. 6 servings.

Photograph for this recipe on page 176.

Sour Cream Sauce for Beef Patties (below)

SOUR CREAM SAUCE FOR BEEF PATTIES

1/2 c. sliced green onions	1 c. sour cream
1 c. sliced fresh mushrooms	1 tbsp. chopped parsley
2 tbsp. butter	Salt to taste

Saute the green onions and mushrooms in butter until onions are slightly transparent, but not brown. Reduce heat to low and add the sour cream, parsley and salt. Simmer until heated through, stirring constantly. Serve over beef patties. About 1 1/2 cups sauce.

HAMBURGER SAUCE

1 1/2 tbsp. Worcestershire sauce	1/2 c. catsup
1/4 c. vinegar	1/2 c. water
3 tbsp. sugar	1/2 c. chopped onion
	1/2 c. chopped green pepper

Mix all ingredients in a saucepan and simmer until thickened.

Carolyn Brewton, Huntington, West Virginia

HORSERADISH SAUCE

1 tsp. salt   1 c. sour cream
1/2 c. prepared horseradish

Mix the salt, horseradish and sour cream in a saucepan and heat through. Do not boil. 1 1/2 cups.

Zola Bond, Louisville, Kentucky

ZIPPY HORSERADISH SAUCE

1 pt. heavy cream   1/8 tsp. cayenne pepper
2 tbsp. prepared horseradish   1/4 tsp. paprika
1 tsp. prepared mustard   1/3 c. vinegar
1 tsp. salt

Whip the cream in a bowl until stiff. Fold in remaining ingredients until blended.

Theresa Mann, Vicksburg, Mississippi

OLIVE SAUCE FOR MEAT LOAF

1/2 c. mayonnaise   1 tbsp. chopped pimento
2 tbsp. lemon juice   1 tsp. chopped parsley
1 tbsp. water   2 tbsp. chopped olives

Combine all ingredients in top of double boiler and cook over boiling water until heated through. Pour over meat loaf just before serving. 5-6 servings.

Danora Waterhouse, Sibley, Iowa

PIQUANT SAUCE FOR MEAT LOAF

3 tbsp. brown sugar   1/4 tsp. nutmeg
1/4 c. catsup   1 tsp. mustard

Combine all ingredients in a bowl and mix well. Spread over meat loaf before baking.

Shirley Johnson, Strange Creek, West Virginia

TART SAUCE

1/2 can tomato sauce   2 tbsp. prepared mustard
2 tbsp. brown sugar   1 c. water
2 tbsp. vinegar

Combine all ingredients in a bowl and mix well. Pour over meat loaf before baking.

Mrs. Charles Taft, Amarillo, Texas

ALMOND-MUSHROOM SAUCE

1 tbsp. chopped onion	Pepper to taste
1 c. chopped fresh mushrooms	2 c. beef bouillon
1/4 c. butter or margarine	2 tsp. lemon juice
1/4 c. flour	1/2 c. chopped toasted almonds
1/2 tsp. salt	

Saute the onion and mushrooms in butter in a saucepan until tender. Add the flour and blend well. Add salt, pepper and bouillon and cook, stirring, until thick and smooth. Add the lemon juice and almonds. Serve over beef casserole. 3 cups.

Katie Fuller, Cordell, Oklahoma

FRESH MUSHROOM SAUCE

1/2 lb. fresh mushrooms	1 tbsp. flour
1 sm. onion, chopped fine	1/2 c. meat stock
2 tbsp. minced parsley	1/2 c. sour cream
4 tsp. butter	Salt to taste

Wash the mushrooms and cut in small pieces. Cook the onion, mushrooms and parsley in 1 tablespoon butter for about 20 minutes or until tender. Blend the flour and meat stock, then stir into mushroom mixture. Add sour cream, salt and remaining butter and heat through.

Beverlyann Rupinski, Baltimore, Maryland

SHERRY-MUSHROOM SAUCE

1 6-oz. can sliced mushrooms	3/4 tsp. cornstarch
2 tbsp. butter or margarine	1/4 c. sherry
1/4 tsp. pepper	

Drain the mushrooms and cook in the butter in a medium skillet for 5 minutes or until golden brown. Add the pepper. Combine the cornstarch with sherry and stir into mushrooms. Bring to a boil, stirring. Remove from heat and serve over steak. About 1 cup.

Mrs. Alton Crews, Rocky Mount, North Carolina

NO-COOK BEARNAISE SAUCE

4 egg yolks	2 tbsp. lemon juice
1/2 tsp. salt	2 tsp. minced onion
1/8 tsp. cayenne pepper	2 tsp. minced parsley
1 c. melted butter	1 tsp. dried tarragon

Beat the egg yolks in a bowl with electric mixer at high speed until very thick. Add the salt and cayenne pepper. Add 1/4 cup butter, 1 teaspoon at a time, beating constantly at medium speed. Combine remaining butter with remaining ingredients and add to yolk mixture slowly, beating constantly. Serve immediately with broiled steak, roast beef or beef fondue. 6 servings.

Mrs. Elaine Smith, Yorktown, Virginia

MUSTARD SAUCE

1/4 c. vinegar	1/4 c. tomato soup
1/4 c. sugar	1/4 c. melted butter
1/4 c. prepared mustard	1 egg

Combine all ingredients in a saucepan and mix until well blended. Cook over low heat until thick, stirring constantly.

Mrs. Joan Perry, Rock Hill, South Carolina

PARSLEYED BUTTER

2 tbsp. grated onion	1/4 tsp. dry mustard
2 tbsp. chopped parsley	2 tsp. Worcestershire sauce
1/4 tsp. seasoned salt	3 tbsp. soft butter or
1/2 tsp. pepper	margarine

Combine all ingredients in a small bowl and blend well. Cover and refrigerate until chilled. Spread over steak just before serving. About 1/3 cup.

Mrs. D. W. Griffin, Frederick, Maryland

VERSATILE TOMATO SAUCE

1/4 c. butter or margarine	4 6-oz. cans tomato paste
4 cloves of garlic, minced	1 tsp. dried oregano
1 c. chopped onion	1/4 tsp. dried basil
1/4 c. chopped parsley	1 1/2 tsp. salt
1 1-lb. 12-oz. can whole	1/2 tsp. pepper
tomatoes	

Melt the butter in a large skillet over low heat. Add the garlic, onion and parsley and cook for 5 minutes or until onion is golden. Add tomatoes and liquid and tomato paste and simmer for 30 minutes. Stir in remaining ingredients and simmer for 30 minutes longer. Press through a coarse sieve and discard vegetables. Serve as spaghetti sauce or over hamburgers or veal cutlets. 3 1/2 cups.

Mildred Nettles, Maryville, Tennessee

PIZZA SAUCE

6 lb. hamburger
2 lb. salami, ground
7 c. tomato paste
2 onions, diced

5 lge. sweet pickles, diced
3 tsp. oregano
Salt and pepper to taste

Combine the hamburger and salami in a kettle and cook over medium heat until brown. Stir in remaining ingredients and cover. Simmer for 1 hour, stirring frequently. Pour into quart containers, leaving room for expansion, and cool. Cover and freeze. Thaw and use 1 quart sauce for each pizza. 7 quarts.

Mrs. Wendy Barr, Newport, Kentucky

QUICK SPAGHETTI SAUCE

1 can tomato soup
1/2 can water
1 tsp. chili powder

1 tbsp. instant or chopped onion

Combine all ingredients and simmer for about 10 minutes. Serve with spaghetti and meatballs.

Mrs. Fred Morrison, Star City, Arkansas

ITALIAN SPAGHETTI SAUCE

1 lb. hamburger
1 qt. tomatoes
1 lge. onion, diced
1 tsp. Worcestershire sauce
1 tsp. salt

1 clove of garlic, minced
1 tsp. paprika
Dash of pepper
1/2 tsp. sugar

Mix the hamburger and tomatoes together and let stand for 30 minutes. Add the remaining ingredients and simmer for at least 2 hours or longer.

Rachel C. Billups, Wetumpka, Alabama

BASQUE SAUCE

1/2 lb. hamburger
3 tbsp. fat
2 tbsp. chopped onion
1/2 c. chopped celery
2 tbsp. flour
1 c. water

2 tbsp. chopped green pepper
1/2 tsp. chili powder
1/2 tsp. salt
1/8 tsp. pepper
2 c. cooked tomatoes

Brown the hamburger in the fat in a heavy skillet, then add the onion and celery. Cook until lightly browned. Stir in the flour, then blend in the remaining ingredients. Simmer for 1 hour or longer. Serve over rice, noodles or toast points.

Mrs. Gertrude Hawkins, Orlando, Florida

SPAGHETTI SAUCE TO FREEZE

2 tbsp. olive oil or butter	1/2 c. dry red wine (opt.)
1 lb. ground beef	2 tsp. salt
2 med. onions, chopped	1 bay leaf
1 clove of garlic, minced	1/8 tsp. thyme
1 4-oz. can mushrooms	1/2 tsp. hot sauce
1 1-lb. can tomatoes	1 tsp. Worcestershire sauce
1 6-oz. can tomato paste	

Heat the olive oil in a heavy saucepan, then add the beef, breaking up into small pieces with a fork. Add the onions and garlic and cook until the beef is browned. Stir in the mushrooms with liquid and the remaining ingredients. Simmer for about 30 minutes or until sauce is thickened. Chill quickly by setting pan in cold water or in refrigerator. Spoon into freezer containers and freeze. Place frozen block into skillet or saucepan and heat slowly to serve. May increase recipe 2 or 3 times. Mixture will keep up to 3 months.

Spaghetti Sauce to Freeze (above)

ABBREVIATIONS USED IN THIS BOOK

Cup	c.	Large	lge.
Tablespoon	tbsp.	Small	sm.
Teaspoon	tsp.	Package	pkg.
Pound	lb.	Dozen	doz.
Ounce	oz.	Pint	pt.
Minutes	min.	Quart	qt.

EQUIVALENT MEASUREMENTS

3 tsp. = 1 tbsp.
2 tbsp. = 1/8 c.
4 tbsp. = 1/4 c.
8 tbsp. = 1/2 c.
16 tbsp. = 1 c.
5 tbsp. + 1 tsp. = 1/3 c.
12 tbsp. = 3/4 c.
4 oz. = 1/2 c.
8 oz. = 1 c.
16 oz. = 1 lb.
1 oz. = 2 tbsp. fat or liquid
2 c. fat = 1 lb.

2 c. = 1 pt.
2 c. sugar = 1 lb.
5/8 c. = 1/2 c. + 2 tbsp.
7/8 c. = 3/4 c. + 2 tbsp.
1 lb. butter = 2 c. or 4 sticks
2 pt. = 1 qt.
1 qt. = 4 c.
A few grains = less than 1/8 tsp.
Pinch = as much as can be taken between tip of finger and thumb
Dash = less than 1/8 tsp.

OVEN TEMPERATURES

Temperature (degrees F.)	Term
250-300	Slow
325	Moderately slow
350	Moderate
375	Moderately quick
400	Moderately hot
425-450	Hot
475-500	Extremely hot

INDEX

PHOTOGRAPHY CREDITS: California Beef Council; National Livestock and Meat Board; The R. T. French Company; California Avocado Advisory Board; United Fresh Fruit and Vegetable Association; Accent International; National Macaroni Institute; Angostura-Wuppermann Corporation; Best Foods: A Division of Corn Products Company International; Standard Brands Products: Fleischmann's Yeast, Planter's Peanut Oil; Pineapple Growers Association; Rice Council; Pet, Incorporated; National Dairy Council; Armour and Company; McIlhenny Company; Frozen Potato Products Institute; Pickle Packers International; Spanish Green Olive Commission; Olive Administrative Committee; Apple Pantry: Washington State Apple Commission; Keith Thomas Company; Ralston-Purina Company; California Raisin Advisory Board; American Dairy Association; American Dry Milk Institute, Incorporated; Campbell Soup Company; The Pillsbury Company; Evaporated Milk Association; American Spice Trade Association; American Home Foods: Chef-Boy-Ar-Dee.

Printed in the United States of America.